THE HOPE THAT REMAINS

The Hope That Remains

Canadian Survivors of the Rwandan Genocide

Christine Magill

FOREWORD BY WILL FERGUSON

PREFACE BY RÉGINE UWIBEREYEHO KING

Véhicule Press

Published with the generous assistance of The Canada Council for the Arts, the Canada Book Fund of the Department of Canadian Heritage, and the Chawkers Foundation.

  Canada Council Conseil des arts
for the Arts du Canada

Cover and title design by David Drummond
Cover photograph by Christine Magill
Set in Minion and Filosofia by Simon Garamond
Printed by Marquis Book Printing Inc.

Dépôt légal, Library and Archives Canada and the
Bibliothèque national du Québec, second trimester 2019.

LIBRARY AND ARCHIVES CANADA CATALOGUING IN PUBLICATION

Title: The hope that remains : Canadian survivors of the
Rwandan Genocide / Christine Magill ;
foreword by Will Ferguson ; preface by Régine Uwibereyeho King.
Names: Magill, Christine, author. | Ferguson, Will, writer of foreword.
King, Régine Uwibereyeho, writer of preface.
Description: Includes bibliographical references and index.
Identifiers: Canadiana (print) 20189067470 | Canadiana (ebook) 20189067489
ISBN 9781550655186 (softcover)
ISBN 9781550655247 (EPUB)
Subjects: LCSH: Rwanda—History—Civil War, 1994—Personal narratives.
LCSH: Rwanda—History—Civil
War, 1994—Personal narratives, Canadian. | LCSH : Genocide—Rwanda.
LCSH: Rwanda—History—1994-
Classification: LCC DT450.436 .M33 2019 | DDC 967.57104/310922—DC23

Published by Véhicule Press, Montréal, Québec, Canada
www.vehiculepress.com

Distribution in Canada by LitDistCo
www.litdistco.ca

Distributed in the U.S. by Independent Publishers Group
www.ipgbook.com

Printed in Canada on FSC ® certified paper.

CONTENTS

Foreword

I came to Rwanda across a soccer field in Calgary. My son's coach was from Rwanda, had escaped just before the killings began. We became friends and would later travel to Africa together. Like most Canadians, my notions of the 1994 genocide against the Tutsi of Rwanda were vague and strangely subdued. It had happened a world away, hardly seemed real. But when I visited my friend's village, where his brother's house had been torn down and local Tutsi boys gathered up and chopped down with machetes, it hit me. "Your childhood home is a genocide site." He turned, looked at me, genuinely puzzled. "All of Rwanda is a genocide site," he said.

If, as Stalin reputedly said, "One death is a tragedy but a million is just a statistic," the challenge among survivors of the Rwandan genocide is to keep the humanity of the victims at the forefront, to stop them from disappearing, from becoming merely a number.

I first heard Christine Magill speak at a Rwandan memorial in Calgary. She taught genocide in school, was thoughtful, articulate, respectful. With support from the Chawkers Foundation, I urged her to gather stories of Canadian survivors before they were lost forever. She took it even further, recognizing that the genocide does not define a person. She wanted to give their full story, of life before the killings, during the killings, and after: how they rebuilt their lives, how they came to Canada.

The Rwandan community has lessons to teach us, if we will listen. Lessons about extremism, about scapegoating segments of society—whoever they may be—of pigeonholing people as part of a group instead of treating them as individuals. It is a warning against exhilarating "calls to action" that both excuse and justify acts of violence, regardless of which side of the political spectrum they originate from. There is a human cost to such rhetoric, and no one has immunity. When you judge people based solely on their ethnic or racial background, you erase them as human beings.

Canada's Rwandan community has overcome odds that would destroy the rest of us. These are our neighbours, our friends, our fellow citizens, and the firsthand accounts in this book give us a glimpse into the human side of those horrific events. They are a powerful testament to the resilience of the human heart, of the hope that refuses to die. I would like to thank the survivors for their kindness and courage in sharing these stories.

Will Ferguson
November 11, 2018

Preface

The ten testimonies in this book are powerful narratives re-counted by survivors of the 1994 genocide against the Tutsi in Rwanda. It is very fitting to publish these stories for the twenty-fifth anniversary of the genocide.

. In 1994 the world watched in horror as the violence unfolded in Rwanda. The media's attention then turned to coverage of sports stars, celebrities, and the stock market. These survivors' stories bring the genocide back to the consciousness of the world and offer us another opportunity to learn.

Stories have been described as dangerous companions. Certain stories have the capacity to unsettle the equilibrium of daily life and demand that we view people and issues with new eyes. Such stories refuse to be pushed away; they stubbornly whisper messages about the nature of the world in which we live and our uneasy acceptance of evil that takes the lives of people in different corners of the globe.

The testimonies in this book remind us that life is never normal after the violence ends. The interviewees are candid about their struggles with fear, trauma, depression, anger, bitterness, trust, and forgiveness. Their stories teach us that there was no sudden outbreak of ethnic violence. Political leaders and government institutions, in-cluding schools, had prepared for years to destroy the Tutsi people.

These testimonies also remind us of the resilience, resistance, and human hopes that endure in times of extreme adversity. A common theme is the loving protection parents bestowed upon their children to resist discrimination and to ensure that love would triumph over hatred. As well, these accounts reveal the sheer determination to survive to tell the story. It is through these human qualities and values that the survivors' resilience shines through despite the loneliness, grief, and suffering induced by their traumatic experiences of the genocide. Their ability to pick up the pieces of their lives and move forward is encouraging.

It is not a light task to read this book. Its stories of violence, the loss of loved ones, the destruction of property, physical wounds, and emotional scars are both compelling and harrowing. As a survivor of the genocide myself, I am aware of how painful it can be to recount one's horrors, sometimes with an audience who cannot relate in any way to our lived experiences. I am also certain that much more could have been told by each person interviewed. I commend those who shared their stories for their courage to speak the unspeakable. I also thank the author, who quickly understood the power of humour in the Rwandans she met and who paid attention to those moments during the interviews. Jokes ease the heaviness of living in the aftermath of genocide. In reading these stories, I found myself crying and laughing at the same time. That in itself is healing.

All the survivors in this book currently live in Canada. Their testimonies demonstrate the challenges of starting life anew as refugees in an unfamiliar environment while coming to terms with past traumas. None of the survivors wished to make readers feel pity for their past, though. They remind us all to open our eyes to the ongoing mass violence in places like Syria and the Democratic Republic of the Congo so that we can actively play our part in making the world a safer place for everyone.

Régine Uwibereyeho King

Introduction

Every immigrant who comes to Canada has a story. This book captures ten of them.

In 1994 Rwanda experienced one of the worst genocides in human history. Over the span of a hundred days, an estimated one million people were killed. The word genocide evokes images of violence, chaos, and death, images that are certainly reinforced by Rwandans' testimonies of the horrific slaughter that raged across their nation.

Survivors of genocide have a story to share about what they've undergone, and when these are recorded the focus tends to be on the atrocities they have lived through as well as the devastating loss of friends and family. What's sometimes missed is the remarkable resiliency and fortitude of the human spirit. We don't always hear about their experiences in the aftermath of the genocide: how they've rebuilt their lives, found a way to move forward, or achieved some degree of healing. Despite their harrowing past, most survivors share feelings of hope, forgiveness, and a belief in a better future.

When I began documenting my interviews with Rwandan survivors, this was an element I wanted to incorporate. The goal was to record their testimonies for future generations, but also to share the lessons their personal accounts can convey. When these survivors talk about their childhood and family life, the things they remember are similar to the experiences of children anywhere in the world—the moments of happiness they had with their families, the feeling of being loved. Yet their narratives also highlight how easily people can be manipulated into turning against one another, how differences can be used to divide a society and breed hatred. Just as political leaders, government officials, the army, and the police can become enemies driven and encouraged to kill, so can priests, teachers, friends, neighbours, and even family members.

The ten Rwandan survivors included in this book recount their journey to escape the violence and chaos that overtook their country (some of their names have been changed to protect their privacy). Eight survivors detail their gripping experiences as they tried to stay alive while trapped in a nation of killers. Two left Rwanda before the genocide began, and as they share the events that forced them to flee, their stories highlight the targeted discrimination to which the Tutsi were subjected and the long period of planning and preparation that preceded the mass killings. Both were then faced with the challenge of being outsiders looking in as things deteriorated in Rwanda and their families were massacred.

However, none of the stories end there. Twenty-five years after the Rwandan genocide, the scars are still very real—for these survivors, coping with trauma and rebuilding their lives remains an emotional struggle. They recount memories from after the genocide as well as the difficult decision to leave the known behind and seek a better life in a new country. Their accounts demonstrate strength and courage while also encompassing humorous moments, thoughtful insights, and an overwhelming love and pride for the new nation they now call home.

These stories have altered the way I view not only this great country but the life I lead within it. They've taught me lessons of forgiveness. They've also demonstrated why we must counter divisionism in all its guises; why we must teach our children about love and acceptance. I've been reminded of the fragility of life and how important it is to cherish each moment with those you love. I hope that through these stories you'll be able to reflect on your own life and gain a better understanding of how, even when horror overtakes the world, there is always a glimmer of hope that remains.

An Overview of the
Rwandan Genocide

The Rwandan genocide was neither spontaneous nor the result of a civil war, despite what the international media reported at the time. It was an outcome of close to one hundred years of colonialism and ethnic divisions.

The term genocide was coined by Raphael Lemkin, a Polish Jew, in the early 1940s. Horrified by the actions taken during World War I against Armenians living in the Ottoman Empire, and finding no word that truly captured the atrocity, Lemkin developed the new term by combining the Greek word *genos*, meaning "tribe" or "race," with the Latin *cide*, meaning "killing." As a lawyer, he devoted his life to achieving legal recognition of the crime of genocide. Success came only after World War II and the Holocaust. Lemkin was forced to flee his country, ultimately reaching the United States. While living there he lost most of his family to the same crime that for years he'd been fighting to prevent. In the aftermath of the war, he doggedly pursued the support of diplomats in the newly created United Nations. Eventually, along with the promise to prevent genocide and punish those responsible, the term was adopted and recognized by international law.

Yet every possible effort was made to avoid its use. To describe what was happening in Rwanda as a genocide would have meant an obligation on the part of international community to intervene— and so instead it was referred to as a "civil war," an "ethnic conflict" where "acts of genocide" had occurred.

With no country willing to become involved, the world stood by and watched while yet another genocide took place.

The population of Rwanda, a small developing country in East Africa, consists of three groups: the Hutu (85 percent), the Tutsi (14 percent), and the Twa, a pygmy people who once lived primarily in the forested regions of the country (less than 1 percent). Some historians define the Tutsi and Hutu as ethnic groups that had migrated from different regions of Africa. Others, however, view these terms as social and economic classifications based on wealth and profession, with the Tutsi being the cattle owners and the Hutu the farmers. A Tutsi king ruled the country, and intermarriage between the two groups was common.

Before its colonization, Rwanda was generally a place of peace. The three groups lived in harmony, sharing the same language and culture.

Germany arrived in Rwanda in 1884, during a time when ethnocentrism prevailed, when it was widely believed that white Europeans were the superior race. They quickly claimed the territory and imposed German rule. Owing to their lighter skin, the Tutsi were considered to be more intelligent and "European-like" than their Hutu country-mates, and were thus given greater access to education and more prominent roles in the colony's administration.

When Belgium took control of the country at the end of World War I, the division between the two groups only intensified. Unable to reliably discern an individual's ethnicity, the Belgian colonizers began issuing identity cards in 1926 to more formerly classify Rwandans. The process began by focusing on the perceived physical differences between Tutsi and Hutu, ranking them according to the precepts of eugenics. Charts were made measuring skin colour, nose size, and the shape of facial features. Tutsi were deemed to be tall, with lighter skin and more refined noses; Hutu were defined as being shorter, with wider and larger noses and a darker skin tone.

However, applying these specifications to the broader population proved challenging, and in the end the difference was often reduced to the number of cattle a person owned: if you had ten or more cows you were classified as Tutsi; nine or fewer, and you were considered Hutu. Bribery also played a role—those who had the money would pay officials for Tutsi identity cards. Family members could find themselves divided into different "ethnicities" regardless of their physical appearance. And in the case of intermarriage, the children's ethnicity was based on that of the father.

In an effort to make their colony profitable, the Belgians introduced forced labour—with the Tutsi often obliged to serve as middlemen between Hutu workers and the colonizers. To escape the brutal oppression of the colonial system, many Rwandans fled to such neighbouring countries as Uganda, Burundi, and the Congo. Over time, the preferential treatment of the Tutsi drove an even greater wedge between the two groups.

The end of World War II heralded a broad shift away from old systems of imperial rule as colonies around the world began to call for independence. Rwanda was no different. And with a growing Hutu elite challenging the country's social and political structures, it was clear that if independence were achieved, they would gain control. In 1957 a Hutu Manifesto was written and the Party of the Hutu Emancipation Movement (Parmehutu) was formed. Two years later, in 1959, tensions boiled over when a Hutu uprising, known as the Social Revolution, led to widespread violence that displaced thousands of Tutsi. In the years that followed, Belgian authorities increasingly supported Hutu leaders, who gradually replaced Tutsi in positions of power.

On July 1, 1962, Rwanda was declared an independent republic, with the Parmehutu in charge. In the years that preceded and followed independence, violent attacks targeted Tutsi. In some places they were forced from their communities and driven into undeveloped areas of the country; many fled the country altogether. As time passed the persecution of Tutsi continued: government positions were reserved for Hutu; political opposition was suppressed; and Tutsi students were generally restricted from receiving an education past primary school. Even there they often faced bullying and harassment from Hutu students and teachers alike.

The term *inyenzi*, or "cockroaches," was introduced to describe Tutsi opponents as an infestation plaguing the nation—a common pest that could easily be killed.

In 1973 Juvénal Habyarimana led a military coup and successfully seized control of the country. He would remain Rwanda's president until the beginning of the genocide over twenty years later. Under his rule the country became a one-party state controlled by the National Revolutionary Movement for Development (MRND); although elections were held, he was the only presidential candidate. During his presidency, Habyarimana formed a close relationship with France, which viewed Rwanda as an important ally amid the growing prevalence of Anglophone nations. As a result, while Kinyarwanda remained Rwanda's primary language, French was used by the government and in schools, and thus came to be associated with prestige.

Meanwhile, Hutu extremism continued to grow. Tutsi who'd fled the country found themselves trapped in refugee camps, unable to return to Rwanda but also unable to integrate into their country of residence. In Uganda, many joined the National Resistance Army (NRA) under the leadership of Yoweri Museveni, assisting in a successful campaign to overthrow the ruling Ugandan government. Now trained soldiers and veterans of a civil war, these Rwandan refugees established the Rwandan Patriotic Front (RPF)—a militia group also known as the RPF Inkotanyi, or "fighters who don't give up." Their goal was to one day return to their country.

On October 1, 1990, the RPF made its move and invaded Rwanda, triggering the start of a civil war. France sent in troops to help rebuff the attacks and keep Habyarimana in power. Long a supporter of the extremist government, France felt a vested interest in protecting its investment in the Francophone nation. Tutsi within the country became targets, accused of being sympathizers or supporters of the RPF campaign. Two months after the invasion came the publication of the Hutu Ten Commandments calling on all Hutu to unite in the fight against the Tutsi. The government, along with Hutu extremists, became determined to rid Rwanda of its Tutsi "infestation." They began planning a final solution.

Throughout the next four years, a propaganda campaign of hate was broadcast via radios and newspapers across the country. Hutu were led to believe that a Tutsi conspiracy was underway to attack and kill them, and that heinous crimes were being committed against Hutu women and children. The anti-Tutsi narrative was further propagated in schools and churches; administrators of both institutions compiled lists of who belonged to which ethnicity. The government formed and began training a youth militia branch of the MRND. Known as the Interhamwe—"those who attack together"— they would become responsible for carrying out the ethnic cleansing. Stockpiles of weapons were secured, a significant number of them purchased from France. Around the nation "practice genocides" were carried out in which Tutsi were massacred over two- to three-day periods. International groups called on the government to intervene and stop the killing—but when troops were sent in it wasn't to restore peace so much as to measure the success of the attacks.

In 1992, under international pressure, ceasefire talks began. Although many of President Habyarimana's supporters viewed his participation in these negotiations as a betrayal of the Hutu Power movement, they led to the end of the civil war. The 1993 Arusha Peace Accords, signed by both Habyarimana and the RPF, set forth a new plan for the country: the MRND would share power with the RPF and four other political groups in a provisional government until demo-cratic elections could be held.

Six hundred RPF soldiers were permitted to set up residence at the Centre Nationale de Developpement in Kigali, the country's capital. The United Nations sent a peacekeeping force of twenty-five hundred soldiers under the direction of Roméo Dallaire, the acclaimed Canadian general, to administer the new peace agreement. Leading the United Nations Assistance Mission to Rwanda (UNAMIR) and troops from Belgium, Bangladesh, Ghana, and Tunisia, Dallaire was to monitor the ceasefire, establish a demilitarized zone, and assist with the creation of a transitional government.

And yet, despite the arrival of UN peacekeepers, little progress was made toward full implementation of the Arusha Accords. The training of Interhamwe soldiers continued. A new radio station, the Radio Télévision Libre des Mille Collines (RTLM), broadcast propaganda condemning the accords and maintaining the extremist narrative. Habyarimana, viewed as a traitor by hardliners, became the target of publications that predicted his death.

Dallaire, who was now aware of the extremist movement within the country, was informed of the stockpiled weapons and coming massacre. However, UN officials in New York told him that taking action would violate UNAMIR's mandate; they refused to allow him to raid the weapon caches or otherwise intervene to prevent the genocide. UN soldiers were forced to stand by and watch as the nation descended into a hell worse than any nightmare could conjure.

On April 6, 1994, the plane carrying Habyarimana and Burundi's Hutu president, Cyprien Ntaryamira, was shot down as it flew past the presidential palace. It is widely believed that the attack originated from within the palace walls by Hutu extremists angry at Habyarimana's willingness to compromise with the so-called *inyenzi*.

The incident was also a signal ringing out across the country: Let the killing begin.

To ensure that no one could gain sufficient control to stop the coming genocide, the presidential guard immediately began murdering political moderates. By the next day roadblocks had been set up across Rwanda. The killing of Tutsi gradually spread from Kigali to the surrounding countryside.

After executing the prime minister, the presidential guard next executed ten Belgian peacekeepers—a targeted attack designed to drive peacekeepers and the international community out of the country and prevent any interference.

Prior to the genocide many Tutsi had decided to stay in Rwanda, confident that with the presence of the UN peacekeepers and under the watchful eye of the international community, no harm could come to them. Now they found themselves being abandoned. Thousands of Tutsi refugees had gathered at a Kicukiro technical college serving as headquarters for the Belgian troops. But with the deaths of ten of its soldiers, Belgium ordered the evacuation of all its remaining peacekeeping troops. As the last Belgian vehicle drove off the compound, the Interhamwe moved in, massacring the Tutsi who had placed their faith, and their lives, in the hands of the peacekeepers.

Within two weeks the United Natiòns voted to reduce its peace-keeping forces from 2,500 to 270 soldiers. Many Rwandans believe that if the UN hadn't been in the country before the genocide the death toll would have been much lower: fewer people would have been wooed by a false sense of security; more would have escaped.

Around the nation Tutsi fled to places they viewed as secure, including churches and schools; local representatives often encouraged them to do so. These institutions became the main killing sites: with Tutsi already rounded up, they were easy to massacre. In churches where both Hutu and Tutsi were seeking refuge, Hutu priests would help point out who should be killed.

Gradually the genocide expanded, reaching every corner of the country. Hutu citizens—primed for years with propaganda about the evil Tutsi—joined the action, killing their neighbours and, in some cases, their own family members. Those who refused to kill were often forced to participate, having been threatened with death or the loss of their families, including their children. Fuelled by alcohol and drugs, Interhamwe raped women, killed babies by smashing them against walls, and buried people alive in mass graves. Machetes, a commonly owned farming tool, were turned into killing devices.

Every day, an unprecedented ten thousand people were slaughtered.

The small group of UN soldiers who remained did their best to save as many lives as possible—often by sitting unarmed outside of churches or other buildings, using their sheer blue-bereted presence to turn away killers and rebuff attacks. In mid-May, a month and a half into the genocide, the UN finally agreed to increase the number of troops. It took another six weeks, until the end of June, for any forces to be deployed.

Meanwhile, as the international community stood by, the RPF launched an immediate offensive. Under the leadership of Paul Kagame they fought their way across the country, establishing safe zones and rescuing anyone found alive. From Kigali they ran rescue missions into extremist-controlled areas in order to evacuate those hiding in compounds such as Centre St. Paul and churches such as St. Famille.

As the RPF gained control of the country, many Hutu, fearing retaliation for their crimes, fled to surrounding nations. The international community turned its attention to the stream of refugees, sending aid and establishing refugee camps for the two million displaced Rwandans. In many cases it was this exodus that became the focus of media attention, with little notice paid to the real event that was taking place. In some of these refugee camps, Hutu extremists continued to target or execute Tutsi survivors.

On July 4, 1994, after nearly a hundred days of slaughter, the RPF seized control of Kigali and began restoring order to the nation. This date later came to be celebrated as Liberation Day, considered a more significant celebration than that of the country's independence.

Rwanda was now a wasteland of bodies. Each river, lake, and road was littered with decomposing corpses. Dogs and other animals that were found eating the bodies had to be destroyed.

The nation faced monumental challenges. With well over a million people implicated in the killings, bringing those responsible to trial presented a seemingly impossible task. The years that followed were spent rebuilding, seeking justice through both international courts and the *gacaca*, or community courts, and figuring out how to move the country forward from the horror of the genocide.

Today, Rwanda is a starkly different place. The ethnic classifications and identity cards have been officially eliminated; the focus now is on a united country. Efforts are being made to raise a new nation of educated citizens—free from the divisions of the past, from the ideology of hatred. Reconciliation remains a major theme, with a goal to prevent the tragedies of the genocide from marring future generations.

Transformation takes time. Tensions persist in the undercurrents of the nation, with detractors criticizing the tight restrictions on the media and the lack of political opposition. And yet, regardless of its critics, Rwanda remains poised to become the success story of East Africa. In 2018 it was ranked number one in the political representation of women, who held 61 percent of government seats. Rwanda has worked to combat poverty and improve education, and has gained international recognition for its continued economic growth and level of government transparency.

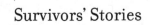

Survivors' Stories

One

Innocent

My first introduction to Innocent came in 2011, at the annual commemoration event for the Rwandan genocide; he was one of the organizers. Although I didn't know much about him, my initial impressions were of a happy university student with a quiet, unassuming presence. Innocent had an air about him that just radiated niceness. When he smiled his entire face would beam; it felt like rays of sunshine lighting up the room. Never did I think that this could be someone who'd lived through genocide. Nor did he fit the stereotype of a Tutsi—he wasn't tall or statuesque and had none of their other defining physical characteristics.

Throughout the interviews I conducted, I found that it was often hard to reconcile the person I was talking to with the story he or she shared. How could someone live with such a passion for life, with such kindness and empathy for others, after surviving such horrendous trauma? Innocent is an example of the resilience of human nature, and of how so many genocide survivors have centred their present-day lives on careers and pursuits that help others.

Four years after meeting Innocent, I had the good fortune to be in Rwanda at the same time he was there visiting his wife. They welcomed me into their home, and in typical Rwandan fashion offered me food and drink. I laughed when Innocent told me he'd brought Crystal Light to make juice with, and had even tried bringing Tim Hortons coffee but couldn't find a small enough container.

During my visit Innocent invited me to a family wedding. It was an incredible experience—a mix of Western and Rwandan traditions. Innocent and his wife even helped me shop for a *umushanana* (the traditional ceremonial dress for women) and jewellery to wear. He sat next to me whenever possible, explaining the meaning behind different traditions and translating from Kinyarwanda, the national language, and French, a legacy of Rwanda's Belgian colonizers. I teased him about how many relatives he had, since every time he introduced me to someone it was either a brother or a cousin. It seemed as though he was related to half the people there. But for Innocent, as for many Rwandans, familial terms aren't reserved solely for those related by blood; they're also used for those you consider family.

This was especially true after the genocide. Households often consisted of the remaining survivors from an extended family, with cousins, siblings, grandparents, and aunts and uncles living together and operating as a family unit. Many people took in and raised children who had been orphaned. Survivor organizations grouped unrelated children into family structures to ensure they would have a source of support and encouragement. These bonds and relationships were essential for their survival.

Knowing that, like me, Innocent believed in the need to document survivors' stories for future generations, he was the first person I contacted about an interview. Innocent has shared his testimony with school groups, university classes, and as part of a living library project. It's a powerful way to help ensure that people learn about what happened in Rwanda, and to encourage them to fight the roots of hatred.

Innocent's testimony is heart-wrenching. I'd heard fragments of it over the course of our friendship, but never the full story. It's difficult to comprehend the maturity with which he shouldered his responsibilities at such a young age and the complicated journey his life took after the genocide.

The interview was not without warm and happy moments. Like a typical Canadian, I wanted to know how Innocent reacted when he first saw snow. He told me that he'd run outside—he'd seen the ice crystals falling from the sky and wondered how they'd feel. When I asked what that was like, he smiled that warm, contagious smile of his and said, "Wonderful."

Innocent's Story

In the 1950s and early 1960s the country began to move towards independence. There was conflict throughout the country, and killings took place targeting Tutsi. In 1959 my parents were forced to relocate by the government in a program designed to displace them from their homes. They had to move to an area that was a forest, where they had to clear the land and start from scratch to make a living. It was much different from the area where they had lived prior to that, and made life much harder. This is the area they were living in when I was born, the seventh child of nine siblings. Despite the challenges we faced, my childhood was a happy and warm time where I was always surrounded by family.

As a child, I didn't know anything about my assigned ethnicity until I started to attend primary school. At one point a teacher asked for Tutsi students to stand up and then for Hutu students to stand up, and I didn't know who I was. I saw some of my friends standing up, and I remained sitting. At the time I was very confused: I didn't know if I should sit together with Hutu children, my friends, or if I was supposed to stand with Tutsi. I didn't know exactly who I was, and that was a challenge. Neither my parents nor my siblings had taught me what ethnicity I was. Having gone through hardships themselves as a result of their identity, I suspect they did not want to tell me such stories, especially at such a young age. They wanted me to be happy and to enjoy my childhood.

April 6, 1994

I remember the night the president's plane was shot down. I was at home with my family; I was only nine years old, and the mood was sombre. Different neighbours came by our house to discuss the plane crash. There was a strong feeling that this was not going to turn out right, and a sense that everyone knew what would happen next.

Around eight p.m. my aunt came to our house. She wanted to take me with her to a place she felt was safer. I still didn't know what was going on. I was old enough to know that people were worried, but I didn't really understand the specifics of what was happening. Families who owned radios would have guests every evening to listen to the news together—it was the only source for news on what was happening in the country. Often when we were listening to the radio I would hear words like "*inyenzi*," "Tutsi," "Hutu," and the playing of songs that would praise some and undermine others. I knew that something was not okay, but I couldn't have imagined the events that happened next.

I left with my aunt, not knowing where we were going, but found it strange that we were going for a long walk so late at night. My aunt, her daughter, maid, and myself left on foot and walked on the main road, since there were no cars running that late at night. Very few people even owned cars in our community, and those who had vehicles did not want to use them to escape, as they would be too easily noticed. It was a very dark night, and being in a rural area there were no streetlights, so it was possible to move without being seen.

It was a strange experience going with her and leaving my parents behind. She alluded to the fact that something was coming; she didn't know for sure what it was, but she had a bad feeling. My other siblings stayed with my parents. I didn't know when I would meet them again, but when you go somewhere you always have the expectation that you will return.

The journey with my aunt was around eight kilometres; we walked until we arrived at Lake Mugesera. She had a friend who lived there and had a boat, and my aunt was positive that they would assist us in crossing the lake. However, when we arrived, the family, who was Hutu, had already left their home. With nowhere else to go, we stayed overnight in the backyard behind their house. I spent the night thinking about my family, wondering how my sister and my brothers were doing and where they were.

I learned later that four of my brothers and my only sister were killed, as were my parents. That is how things went.

Early in the morning when the sun began to rise we went to hide ourselves in a patch of nearby sorghum bushes. It was the rainy season and the sorghum crops, which were a staple crop in Rwanda, were flowering and provided dense coverage for hiding. I did not really understand what was happening or why we were hiding.

After many hours, people began to arrive in the area and search for Tutsi to kill. One man approached our spot and was trying to uproot cassava roots for food. We knew he was with a group of men because we could hear them talking to one another. When he spotted us in the bushes, he let out a shout. The baby in my aunt's arms, who was around three years old, started to cry. I jumped up and ran to a nearby water dike that was covered by bushes and hid myself there.

The man who had spotted us called for the others to join him. My aunt's maid was Hutu; she was recognized by these people and taken by them. My aunt and her daughter were both slaughtered by the men. I could hear the sounds of them being killed from where I was hiding.

After the men finished the killing they came looking for me. They wandered the area, trying to find some trace of where I had gone or was hidden, but couldn't seem to find me, or see me in the dike where I was hidden. That's how I survived.

I stayed there for a long time, probably even longer than I had to. I did not know when they left. I stayed there for maybe two hours before I climbed out to see what was going on around me. I felt traumatized from what I had listened to. I had heard everything during the attack, all the cries of my niece and my aunt as they were killed. I did not have the courage to go and see what they had done with my aunt. I knew she had been killed, but I could not bring myself to look and see if they had left her corpse or that of her daughter. I now knew what was going on, and that the fears of my parents and neighbours had come true.

I started to find my way back home. It wasn't easy because on the way I could see that people had just been killed and houses were on fire. I knew the place well, as it was the way I would usually pass when I went to school. The school I had attended was nine kilometres from my home and I would walk there every morning, so I was very familiar with the area and was able to stay in the bushes, away from the road. When I glimpsed the road, I could see that it was full of military vehicles and Interhamwe who were on their way to kill people.

Along the way, I saw one of my relatives lying on the road. It wasn't the right thing for me to see at the beginning of this catastrophe, and especially not as a young child. It is a moment that I will never get past and that continues to traumatize me.

It was the body of my uncle's wife lying on the ground. Those who had killed her were still there; I could hear them speaking from the bushes. Her young daughter, who was very small, just recently born, was still alive and lay crying on her chest. I didn't know what to do. I could see and hear the baby, but I couldn't do anything to help her. What was I to do? In the end, I turned and kept walking. I could not save the baby; there was nothing I could do.

The image of this scene has haunted me and played over and over in my mind ever since. It is the moment and image that I always associate with the genocide. It is something that over time I have had to reconcile with myself and accept and take in. I kept this image to myself for more than twenty years before finally finding the courage to tell my uncle. He listened to me and said it was good that I had told him, but that there was nothing I could have done and not to blame myself. It is good that he now knows of that incident—that someone saw where his wife was that day, and where she might have fallen.

After this occurred, I continued on. It was hard to find a way to stay safe amidst the chaos and the killers hunting for victims. Somehow by luck, or by grace, I made it safely back to my family's neighbourhood. When I got close to where my home was, I met a few other people who had also survived that day. I say "few" because most of them had lost their parents and siblings, and only a very few had survived. I spotted a classmate of mine and asked him if he knew what was going on, and he told me about what had happened. This is when I came to learn that my parents and many of my siblings had been killed. I found out that one of my brothers had also gone missing. No one knew of his whereabouts until I saw him again after the genocide and found out that he had been taken hostage by the killers.

That evening, those of us who were still alive gathered in the forest. At this gathering I was relieved to see that two of my older brothers had survived. It became a regular thing in the days that followed; those of us who were still alive would meet up every evening. It was an odd sort of routine to give us strength to continue the next day. During daylight we would go into hiding, sometimes individually, sometimes in groups or as families. I occasionally hid with my brothers, but eventually I considered everyone still alive to be my brothers and sisters and would hide with different groups or by myself. We were not well organized, as sometimes we had to flee quickly from killers, all heading in different directions. That happened to me twice. We were attacked and had to split up and flee, but I was fortunate and survived both these incidents. In the evenings when we gathered, deep in the night, we would see who had made it through, and then we would cook whatever food we may have found and eat it together. You didn't think of the future—there was never any guarantee you would survive. You just hoped and prayed day by day.

I never went back to my house again. All the houses had been demolished. Those that were thatched had been burned down, and those with iron sheets had been taken away by people scavenging for them. Everything was scattered. Life was to be hoped for, but at the same time we didn't have any life to hang on to. Much of the catastrophe in my area happened in the first week of the genocide. That is when our neighbours and the trained extremists started going around and killing everyone who was known to be Tutsi or a Tutsi sympathizer.

In the second week there was a defence by Tutsi men who had survived but had some of their children and wives killed. They wanted to die fighting—in hopes that they could fend off the killers and secure the place. It was an impossible task, as they had no weapons. No one knew this was coming, so no one was prepared for war. The planning to exterminate Tutsi took place in the shadows. The defence didn't stand a chance and was ended very quickly.

I stayed in the area near my neighbourhood, but at times the killers knew or suspected that my friends and I had survived and were still living in that area. One rainy afternoon they tried to locate us, but we heard them coming and scattered. The elders among us had been cooking food for all of us to eat. The killers took the barrels they had been using for cooking and scooped dirt inside. When the killers left and we returned to our gathering place we saw that the food was gone, and we knew they were after us. After this we took to sleeping in different places: some groups in one house, and some in another. Though the houses were missing their roofs or partially destroyed, we would still find a way to gain some shelter from the buildings. It was rainy season, so whatever shelter we could find was helpful in providing some protection from the weather.

While in hiding I also saw my uncle; it was his wife who had been killed and left on the road with the baby. I didn't tell him about seeing his wife or baby. I was still too traumatized. He had four sons with him, one who was eleven, one who was a year younger than me (eight years old), and a set of six-year-old twins. The younger children went with him every morning when he was in hiding.

One evening when we gathered, he arrived with the children. They had been injured: the twins and the eight-year-old had been cut with machetes on their heads and their ears. The next day one of the twins didn't come back. No one asked my uncle about it. He knew what had happened—whether the young boy was found and killed, or whether he died in the woods—but we didn't ask him. The other three boys survived the genocide and are still alive today, but the younger two continue to suffer from the machete wounds that were inflicted on them.

Sometime around May 10th, the RPF [Rwandan Patriotic Front] arrived. They were recognized by some of those in hiding because of the different languages they were speaking. The RPF communicated in Swahili and English, languages that were not common in Rwanda, and generally only used by businessmen. Those who were first reached by the RPF assisted the soldiers in finding others who were also in hiding. As a result, the soldiers were able to rescue large groups of people. We were reached in May, and taken first to the location of a former market. We spent one night at this place, but early in the morning a bomb was thrown towards the camp. After that we were lined up on the road and taken to a different market space, where the RPF had constructed a more secure camp to help ensure the safety of the survivors. For the remainder of the genocide I stayed in this secured RPF camp with my two brothers.

In total there were only fifteen hundred to two thousand survivors in my district. Some people also died after the genocide, from the injuries inflicted upon them or from the conditions in which they survived. An estimated thirty-five hundred people were killed in the district, based on the bodies found and excavated. However, there are those who threw themselves into lakes or rivers, opting to drown rather than face the pain of being killed by machetes, and not all of those were counted. Bodies continue to be found in Rwanda every year, so it is impossible to ever have exact numbers of the total that perished.

* * *

The whole purpose and intent of the genocide was to exterminate everybody who was Tutsi. Some people lived through the whole genocide period—for three months, a hundred days. I stayed in it for a month, and I don't know what would have happened if I hadn't been saved by the RPF. The way I lived for that month, constantly hiding and being afraid, did not leave me for a long time. Even after the genocide ended and trials were being held for the killers, my thoughts continued to focus on this idea of surviving just one more day. I lived, but I don't know how it happened. I look at myself and look at other people who also survived there, and I don't know what category of life we existed in. It is a miracle that we continued to live.

After the genocide I stayed with my uncle and my cousins, the same ones I saw during my month in hiding. We learned to do many different things together, and tried to live as a family. We learned to prepare meals together and care for the six-year-old. But my uncle was traumatized and became an alcoholic, drinking whenever he could get a hold of anything. No one who survived was in their right mind; everyone was traumatized and trying to find some way of healing. I still don't think healing has fully taken place. At the commemorations every year, you see people who refuse to come because of the trauma, and many of those who do come are seized by memories and emotions and have nightmares or break down crying. The experience and trauma is something that doesn't go away, and I don't think it ever will, or that it should.

Life continued like this for us until the year 2000. One night, one of my other uncles was riding his bike back from visiting his son at boarding school when he was attacked and killed. We heard the story in the morning, when his body was discovered. His son was also attacked—cut in the head with a machete and left for dead. His skull was fractured, and he sustained brain damage and severe trauma. He has been left with permanent scars, which he attempts to cover by wearing hats. He has also been left with cognitive challenges and extensive, ongoing trauma.

After this event, my older brother decided that we must leave Rwanda. My brothers, cousins, and I went to an area where the long-distance trucks park. There were five of us in total, and my brother was desperate to get us all out of the country. We found a driver who was going to Kenya and was willing to take us. He took us to Nairobi, the capital of Kenya, by hiding us inside a shipping container on the back of his truck.

We didn't know anyone in Nairobi, but with everything that had happened we were thankfully able to claim refugee status with the United Nations. Our first challenge was to learn Swahili, which is the main language spoken in Kenya, and then English. We were supported by organizations there that helped us with food and clothing. Often we acted as each other's parents, taking care of one another. All of us were able to go to high school in Nairobi, and I did some vocational training. Eventually, through the United Nations, we received refugee status from the Government of Canada.

In 2008 we left Kenya and travelled first to New Brunswick, then, after a few months, on to Alberta.

The first surprise and source of excitement when coming to Canada was the experience of flying in a plane for the first time. I was awe-truck while boarding, as I couldn't believe that I would soon be sitting in the sky.

The second big surprise was the snow. I was in our apartment in New Brunswick, and at around five or six a.m. I saw these small white, clear crystals falling. I immediately ran outside to see them. I wanted to know what snow felt like, and if it would hurt when it touched me. When I felt my first snowflake I was in awe. I loved it. At the time it was not that cold, so I thought that it must always be like this when it snowed. I started wishing for snow every day, believing it to be a wonderful thing. Snow comes, it's beautiful, but not too cold to eat. To my surprise it started to get colder, first minus ten, then minus twenty. That's when my ears and my fingers began to feel itchy and to hurt. After that I started to think differently about the snow, and it lost some of its magic. Eventually I came to see that this weather was a normal condition of life, which people are used to here, so I became better adjusted to the cold temperatures.

It was during this winter season that I first went to church in Canada. In the past I had been very involved in the church, and had worked as a missionary in Kenya. In Fredericton, some new friends came to meet us to go to church with them. It was like nothing I had ever experienced before. I had never been to a place where there was a mixture of people from all different ethnicities, colours, cultures, and backgrounds, all of whom were gathered and praying together and expressing the same reverence for God. I loved it, and it showed me a new view of the world. If people from so many different backgrounds could pray together and create an inclusive community, then it was also possible to have an inclusive, well-organized, loving, and neighbourly country. This is something I had never experienced before, and I was amazed that a place like this could exist in the world.

This is something that I love about Canada, and why I have loved living here. I love the policy of multiculturalism, the human rights, and the diversity—the fact that these are seen as strengths in our nation and encouraged instead of being used as a way to divide people. I also appreciate the system of government, the leadership, and the benefits and freedoms of living in a democracy.

Injustice is going on to this day in countries around the world. People have the potential for both the good and the bad in them, and as long as they don't live focusing on the good, injustice will continue. Each person should live embracing the good in them to create a mutually accepting society which is suitable for all. If they do this, they will focus on what is good and what will be beneficial for them, their friends, and fellow citizens, and avoid that which is bad in the world. Some may say that my views are that of a pacifist, but these are the beliefs I have after surviving the genocide. Rather than focusing on an ideology, people must find a common ground on which they can solve their differences and live together to see their future. Then society will be much better—we will respect one another and live in peace.

I think Rwanda is also on its way to development; they are making strides day by day to achieve and to do great things for citizens. People are focusing more on what can help them achieve economic stability. On the side of justice, there are now laws enforced to help keep people in check and the country safe. It's my hope that the country achieves long-term stability so that citizens will no longer have to worry about the future. They must find a formula by which people learn to live together and accept one another, and this will change the generations that follow.

Now here in Canada, I am involved in many different things, which fulfill my passions. I work in a church, with people from Rwanda and Burundi. I also work with people from Kenya, Tanzania, and Uganda, who speak Swahili. It has become an advantage that I speak fluent Swahili and many local East African languages. I also volunteer with my local Rwandan community and with a national Rwandan organization. On top of that I have a full-time job, and take some classes as a university student.

All this comes together to explain the whole of me. I am a proponent and advocate of a society which is inclusive, which is harmonious, and which looks out for the benefits of one another.

[Two]

Ruth

I met Ruth through some Rwandan friends I'd known for close to ten years. When I reached out to her, not only did she agree to be interviewed, but she also found two other survivors who wanted to participate in the project. I flew out to Manitoba, taking the opportunity to visit the Human Rights museum in Winnipeg—a stark reminder of how often human rights have been violated and ignored over the last two hundred years. And yet, as I worked my way through each floor, it was also a reminder of hope, of the many people and organizations that have come together to fight for change.

It's a fight that's currently going on in Rwanda as the nation works to rebuild and redefine itself. Children are taught that citizens are simply Rwandans—that the Hutu–Tutsi ethnic divisions were arbitrarily enforced and that such distinctions don't actually exist. Unity clubs in schools encourage students to fight prejudice and discrimination. It's a challenging process, however, especially when so many of their elders have been traumatized and continue to suffer from PTSD.

Many survivors like Ruth have turned to faith as a way to find healing. In her case it has allowed her to forgive and move forward with her life. Although sharing her survivor testimony was emotional and challenging, Ruth's rediscovered joy for life was evident. Our time together ended up being my favourite experience of the summer.

We'd delayed our interview by one day after Ruth had found out she'd be receiving her Canadian citizenship. When I arrived the next afternoon, her excitement about having attended the citizenship ceremony with her family and friends was obvious. She even had a photo ready to show me—and when I saw the pride she had for her new country, it made me proud to be a Canadian.

I was welcomed like family. Ruth had homemade Rwandan soup on the stove, and insisted that before anything else we sit down together and eat. Her apartment was full of life; I could feel the warmth and love that resonated within its walls. Over the course of our visit I met Ruth's children, her husband, one of her best friends, and her friend's two daughters. It reminded me so much of how, in Rwanda, it's the bonds with friends and family that are the true measure of wealth, not how nice your things are or how fancy your home.

Despite having to share sad, difficult experiences, throughout the interview Ruth kept finding moments to smile and laugh. For many, this is the only way to avoid the anger and depression that comes from thinking and talking about the genocide. We also found some comic relief in the exploits of her friend's toddler, who regularly tried to steal away the audio recorder. Ruth's husband joined us partway through, providing more laughter and a chance to ask how he'd ever convinced Ruth to marry him after she'd turned down multiple other proposals.

Most of the interview was done in Kinyarwanda, with Ruth's son and her friend helping to translate. Afterwards, Ruth and her husband insisted that I stay for dinner. They'd cooked traditional Rwandan food; everything was delicious. When they saw how much I'd dished up they jokingly threatened to call my Rwandan friends (the ones who'd connected us) and report me if I didn't eat more. By the time I left that evening, they felt like family. I was sad to go.

Ruth's Story

I grew up in a family of seven children, but one passed away before the genocide, leaving six of us. As a child I didn't know anything about the ethnic divisions in the country. Then in school one day the teacher asked those who were Tutsi to stand up. I stayed seated, and the other children in the class pointed at me and said, "You are Tutsi. We know your family." We lived in a community where everyone knew one another, and Tutsi families were in the minority. I went home that day and told my family what had happened. I asked what all this was about, and they explained that on identity cards it lists your tribe: Hutu, Tutsi, or Twa.

When it was time to transition to high school, most Tutsi wouldn't be admitted to the government schools—they could only continue if they could afford to attend a private high school. So I moved to Kigali to live with my older brother, and began working.

My brother had a shop where he sold items he had imported. Originally he sold rice, sugar, and various drinks, but from there he transitioned to second-hand clothes and then the metal poles used for construction. He had five trucks as part of the business, and altered what we sold based on the clients we had. When I went to work with him I became the manager of the shop. I had a good head for business and was very organized. It worked well, as he liked to move around and handle other aspects of the company, so this ensured that someone was always looking after the shop. I was young but he trusted me the most, even though there were three other siblings between him and me. He knew I was skilled at business and that he could trust me to look after things even when he wasn't there. If anyone came to the shop to ask him questions, he would always direct them to me; I was in charge.

When I first went to work for him we lived near the shop. I performed a lot of the household chores, like cooking and cleaning. Later on, when he got married, I expected that things were going to change because he was starting a new life with his wife. He built a house, but he added a basement just for me, with a bedroom and a bathroom. He wanted me to continue to live with him and be a part of his family.

When I met my husband and decided to get married, my brother was very sad. He told his wife, "I wish she was born a boy," because back then, when a girl got married she would leave and move into the home of her new husband. Even after I got married I continued to be involved in the business, but with fewer responsibilities.

I got married at the age of thirty-two, which was quite late by Rwandan standards. My husband lived in the same areas as us, and even though we were not friends, we knew of each other. He was a very quiet man who didn't talk much. I don't know why he decided to ask me.

At the time when my husband asked me out I had many friends and was very popular. Working in the shop, I would always be meeting people, both men and women. I was very friendly and outgoing, and when my friends faced problems they would confide in me. I heard so much about the challenges and struggles of their marriages that I was determined not to rush into it. Many boys had proposed to me in the past, but I always said no. My life was good; I didn't face any challenges; I had money and a good family. I didn't want to change that by marrying the wrong person, and had decided I would wait until I found a good man.

At this exact point in our interview, almost as if on cue, Ruth's husband walked in the front door and we all burst out laughing.

When he asked me out I was a bit unsure if it was a good idea. He came and met my family and my brother. They told me he was a good guy and would be a really good husband. My brother, whose opinion I valued the most, also approved. This opened my eyes. I decided to give him a chance, and I am so glad I did.

We were married in 1993, and continued to live in the same area, the Kicukiro district of Kigali, near my family. It was a very difficult time in the country. Over the past few years things had deteriorated and ethnic divisions had worsened. In 1990 the RPF had invaded Rwanda, worsening the situation. In 1992 my brother was driving his car when a rock was thrown at him, breaking the car window and hitting him in the head. A week after the incident, he decided to move to Kenya. He took his wife and children and asked me to go with them. I decided to stay in Rwanda to care for our parents. When things calmed back down in our region, they came back to Rwanda and were there for my wedding.

In February of 1994 I was pregnant and expected to give birth that month. At six p.m. one evening, people showed up at my house with machetes and guns and broke into the home. My maid saw them and screamed. My husband attempted to close the door to block them, but they pushed him out of the way and yelled at him to lie on the floor. They beat him while he lay there. I tried to run to my room to lock myself in, but they were faster than me. They held a machete to my head and demanded money. I was still working with my brother and had money that I was supposed to deposit at the bank. I gave this to them. They looked around for anything else that was valuable and took it with them. Before they left they locked us in the house and took the keys so that we couldn't leave. Thankfully we had spare keys, and after they left we were able to get out. [Door locks in Rwanda are designed so that they can be locked with a key from either side.]

The event was so traumatizing that I miscarried the baby. I was feeling poorly and went to the hospital, and that is how I found out that the child had died. From that point on I became terrified anytime I saw someone I wasn't expecting. I always feared the worst.

APRIL 6, 1994

The night the president's plane was shot down I was at home. We heard gunshots but didn't find out that the president had died until the next day. They announced on the radio that no one was

44

allowed to leave their homes. We felt trapped—that all we could do was sit and wait to die. There were soldiers going up and down the street, stopping at the houses. We had a houseboy, and he tried to open the gate a little bit to see what was going on outside. Right after he opened it the soldiers saw him and demanded to see his ID card. Luckily he was Hutu, and when they saw that they assumed that everyone in the house was also Hutu. They asked him, "Tell us where the Tutsi live—in this area where do the Tutsi live?"

He replied, "I don't know any of the Tutsi." The soldiers moved on to the next house. They took a Tutsi man from that home and shot him on the road in front of our gate. This ended up protecting us because when other soldiers passed by they saw the blood near the gate and assumed that our house had already been done. God was protecting us at that time. They went into every single house, but for some reason they didn't enter ours.

The homes were searched on April 7th, which was a Thursday. Two days later, on the Saturday, the chairperson for the region announced that there would be a community meeting. He called it a "Peace Meeting" so that everyone felt it was safe to attend. In reality they wanted everyone to come out and gather so that they could see who had died and who still needed to be killed. My husband went to the meeting, and this made them aware that he was somehow still alive, even though he was on the list of those to be killed.

On Sunday the Interhamwe came to our house and discovered we were all still alive. The soldiers arrived armed with weapons and holding grenades. There were eight of them—they had red eyes and looked as if they had gone mad. I thought, "This is it."

They demanded we exit the house so that they could search it. They went through and checked everything, even the books on the shelves. They were looking for money, but more importantly, to see if we had any connection to the RPF. We were very scared. We knew people who had left and were part of the RPF, and on occasion they would visit us, so we were very worried they would somehow find this out.

I told them I would give them money, and they asked how much I had. I had $5,000. They said they would take the money, along with the documents and pictures they had found in the house. The leader of the group told us they would come back later to kill us. I said to the soldiers, "Please don't kill us. We haven't done anything to you guys."

They returned at eight p.m. This time there were only two soldiers. One of them had been part of the group in the morning. He told us, "You guys? I can't believe you're still alive. I have to kill you. You are Tutsi—you are not supposed to be living still."

The second man said, "You know? Maybe just leave them alone. These people ... Why are we supposed to kill them anyway?"

The first man looked at me and my husband and said, "You guys are extremely lucky. Your wife, this morning, she looked at me and said, 'Why are you killing us? Please leave us alone.' And I felt like something held me back. This has never ever happened to me before. You should consider yourself one of the luckiest people in the whole world because I have never experienced anything like this in my entire life. I don't know why this happened. I can't figure out what it is about your wife that is stopping me. I kill, that's what I do, I kill." He basically said he'd leave us alone, and the two men left. I didn't know if this would last long, but it had to be God or an angel that protected us from that man.

A few days later, around April 14th, the RPF reached the area where we lived and began visiting each home to see if there was anyone they could rescue and transport to a safer location. They didn't discriminate by ethnicity; they were helping everyone, both Hutu and Tutsi. The RPF wanted to move everyone out of the area, away from the fighting.

Trying to move people between regions was very dangerous. There were no vehicles to transport people. The RPF led a large group of us out of the area, trying to avoid places where there were government military forces. Everyone had to walk and try to stay hidden. There was fighting going on in the area between the RPF soldiers and the government soldiers. Many people in the group were killed from the shooting going on around us. In a way it was still much better than many other places, because the RPF reached us so soon. For people in other parts of the country, it took a long time before they were reached by the RPF and could be rescued.

We had left during the night. They took us to the only place that was safe at the time, the CND [Centre Nationale de Developpement], where the RPF troops were stationed, inside Kigali. We arrived early in the morning. The conditions were very poor; it was difficult to even find drinking water. They divided us into family-like groups, especially the women, and served us food that way, to try and make things easier. There were so many of us, but there were no homes or proper resources to care for everyone.

As days passed and they gained control of more areas, they would visit homes and ask families to take people in and care for them as a short-term solution. They would also use homes abandoned by families who had fled the area, or where the families had been killed, to temporarily house people.

I had only been there for one night when in the morning some RPF soldiers came looking for me. When they had been checking houses, they visited the home of my older brother, the one who had owned the shop. He and his entire family had been killed except for one son, named Jean-Paul. The killers had left him there thinking he was going to die, because he was so severely injured. For some reason God saved his life. The maid who lived with them had also survived. The killers had tortured her, but she hadn't been killed. When the RPF came she told them, "That little boy is still alive. The rest of the family is gone, but I think Jean-Paul is still alive." The RPF had brought Jean-Paul to a section for injured people at the CND, and wanted me to be close by to help care for him. He had been shot and was not able to do anything for himself.

We remained there for a week. The fighting was continuing around us. Government soldiers kept shooting at us, so the RPF decided to evacuate everyone. They moved us to Byumba, the province closest to Uganda, where we would be safe. The RPF had secured that region at the very beginning of the conflict, so it was safe from attacks by government soldiers.

Even though we were no longer surrounded by fighting, the conditions were still very poor. People were traumatized, wounded, and suffering. We had relatives who lived in Uganda. When they found out where we were, they came and took us home with them.

We returned to Rwanda in August, when the genocide had ended. Even finding anyone still alive that you knew was difficult. When we tried to return to our home, it was unrecognizable. It had been completely demolished. The only house that was still intact was my brother's, which had only the windows and doors removed. We ended up staying with a friend who had also survived. Her home had been lived in by soldiers, so it hadn't been destroyed. We stayed there for about a month before finding a place of our own.

Jean-Paul was still alive but had many wounds and injuries. After we returned I ended up taking him to Nairobi in Kenya, where they were able to perform an operation to help him. He's now fully grown up and is a handsome man. He attended university in the United States, and now lives in Rwanda.

After we returned I heard how the rest of my family members had died. My dad was killed in front of my parents' house and buried the same day in a very tiny hole. For a long time I was too scared to dig up his body, so instead I put tiles around the grave. Before we moved to Uganda we removed him from there and gave him a proper, dignified burial.

My mother and the other people with her were thrown alive into the Nyabarongo River. Before pushing them in the killers hacked their knee ligaments with a machete to ensure they would drown. I heard that my mom tried to escape the river because she knew how to swim, but they pushed her back in a second time, and she died. My brother who was closest in age to me went to a church, and when they began killings there he tried to escape and hide somewhere else. We know he was killed but were never able to learn the exact place or the location of his body. My other siblings were also all killed, along with their children. The only two members of my family who survived were Jean-Paul and one of my brothers who had been in the U.S. when the genocide began.

After the genocide I was extremely traumatized. I struggled to sleep. From the time I went to bed at night until I got up in the morning, I cried. My bed would be wet with tears. I felt deep sadness and anger and hatred towards the Hutu people. I didn't want to look at them, and refused to speak or interact with them. When I became pregnant again I was terrified. I thought to myself, "I lost the first baby. My whole family is gone. I can't handle this. This baby is going to die too."

I would try to go to church, but even that was too difficult to handle. When I saw people singing I remembered my dead family and thought, "Those people have killed them." I couldn't stand it, and had to walk out. It was too much for me to cope with.

I was sad and depressed all the time. I would say that God did not exist. I would ask, "How come I stayed alive? Why didn't I die? This is not a life. I don't have a life. I'd rather be dead." I didn't want to live. I was very angry.

In March of 1996 a friend invited me to attend church with her. I decided to take a chance and go. The preacher was a man from Kenya. During the service he looked at me and asked that I stand up. I thought to myself, "I'm Tutsi. I don't know this guy. He doesn't know me. Why would I stand? He's probably thinking of someone else." But he continued to insist I stand up, so eventually I got up.

The preacher pointed to me and said, "You think God doesn't love you, that He left you. But He loves you. He knows who you are. Try not to stay angry." Then he prayed for me.

What happened after that is impossible to explain. It felt as though all the hurt and all the burdens I had been carrying were now gone. I felt so much peace.

After that it was as if my eyes had been opened. I started laughing again. I would see the Hutu people, and would feel mercy towards them instead of hatred and anger. I was convinced that I had to forgive. God would start helping me to forgive.

When you are unable to forgive, it kills you. It eats you up on the inside and you are unable to live life. I learned that I couldn't find peace from anything else, or from anyone else. It could only be found through forgiveness.

In 2002 I returned to my hometown in Rwanda with my husband and kids, who were very young at the time. I had hired workers to care for the land and keep the place in good condition, and had arranged to meet with them. The children were running around outside playing while I talked with the workers in the house.

Suddenly a guy walked up to me. He was one of the people who had killed my family. I was caught by surprise and became frightened. I hadn't seen where he was coming from and didn't know he had been released from prison. I knew him very well: he was among those who killed my dad. He said hello and shook my hand.

I looked at him and realized that he couldn't do anything to me, or harm me. Then I forgave him. I knew then that I was completely saved. It was like a test to see if I was capable of fully forgiving. Now I spend my life praising and thanking God because I live a life with joy again.

In 2006 we moved to Uganda. I knew that God had protected me, but sometimes I still worried. Even though I had lost so many people, God had blessed me with children and my husband. There were still extremists in Rwanda, and some were being released from prison. I was afraid that things could happen again and that there could be a genocide in the future. I wanted to ensure that my children were always safe.

We stayed in Uganda for six years before deciding to come to Canada in 2012. It is a country we had heard wonderful things about, and we knew it was safe. There is freedom and security, and it is one of the best countries in the world. I also knew that there would be better opportunities for my children.

Seeing snow for the first time was an interesting experience. I liked it, but I didn't like the cold. The hardest thing was the language. It was also difficult not knowing anybody and feeling isolated. They had given us an orientation in Uganda which taught us about cultural differences. However, the reality is that you really have to experience things to understand them.

The things I miss most about Rwanda are the food and the climate. I was used to eating organic food that we grew ourselves or was grown nearby. This is something I miss from Rwanda and Uganda, where there are no additives. It takes time to adjust. Same with the fruit. I can eat an orange here, but it is not the same as a fresh, organic one in Rwanda. I also miss the beauty of the Rwandan landscape.

There are many things I value about being in Canada. Most of all it is the people. They are the ones that really matter in life and make things good. Whether you are rich or poor, the people around you are the ones who provide you with support and love. When my family and friends are all together I feel such happiness that I don't even know how to thank God for what I have.

We know how to live with so much, but we also know how to live without anything. Here in Canada the government tries its best to ensure that everyone is looked after and cared for. If you lose your job, there are programs to help you. There is health care for everyone. I also appreciate how education is so highly valued in Canada, how there is a public system where everyone can attend. Children are able to go to school from a young age, and also attend high school. In other countries you often have to pay to go to school, and not everyone can afford it.

I like to make sure I thank God every time I eat. Some people think, "Why?" For me it is important. God provides life and food.

I know that some people don't have food. In Africa, sometimes a person can go two days without anything to eat. These are the kinds of things we don't take for granted. Most Canadians, though, don't have anything to compare their lives to, so I can't tell others, "Don't complain," when they talk about this country. I know that the history of Canada also had its difficult and shameful moments to get where we are today. We must always thank God for what we have.

[Three]

Marie

When I first met Marie, I had no idea she was a survivor. Young, vibrant, and stunningly beautiful, she was helping to translate Ruth's story. Marie had brought her daughters with her; the younger of the two, a toddler, stayed with us throughout her difficult, challenging testimony, providing periodic moments of laughter. Marie carries not only psychological scars from having lived through the genocide but physical scars as well, from the machete wounds inflicted upon her. It is remarkable that she survived at all. Ultimately, her story demonstrates the benevolence of the adage "Do unto others as you would have others do unto you."

Like many of the survivors in this book, Marie was a child, at home on Easter break, when the genocide broke out. Boarding schools were (and still are) common in Rwanda; siblings often attended different schools, meaning that families were spread out in different areas of the country. Many people think the timing of the genocide was intentional. The president's plane was shot down three days after Easter Sunday, when most families were still gathered together—making it much easier to kill an entire family at once. In contrast to the Holocaust, where each death was carefully documented, the goal of the Rwandan genocide was to erase any evidence of a person's existence. If no one from that person's family survived to testify, how could anyone be found guilty of killing them?

At the time of the genocide, the majority of Rwandans depended on subsistence farming. And so, once the RPF gained control of the country, people had no choice but to go back to where they'd lived—to salvage whatever was left, and to rebuild. This usually meant returning to the same village, the same house, the same neighbours. To the same place where they'd been targeted, where they'd witnessed the massacre of family and friends. Many of the churches and schools that had operated as killing sites were cleaned up and began holding services and classes again. In some ways everything was the same, but in other ways it was drastically different.

As time passed and prison sentences were served, some of those responsible for the killings also returned to their communities. Your neighbours could once again be the people responsible for murdering your family. Not only were survivors left with the trauma of the genocide; they also faced the daily torture of living in a place where everything, and everyone, served as a reminder. In the years following 1994, this was how Marie and her family lived. What finally changed their future was the decision of a Canadian family to look for a way to help them leave Rwanda.

Many of those who come to Canada as refugees are sponsored by church groups. Churches often play a critical role in raising the necessary funds and then, once the family arrives, providing the long-term support they need. Marie's experience is a testament to the incredible impact these sponsorships can have. She is a proud Canadian who views this country as home, who has a lifelong bond with the church, the community, and the family that supported her. Moving to Canada gave her an opportunity to heal, and to find peace. In Canada she was able to finally begin living her life again.

Marie's Story

When I was growing up I had a good life. We had more than enough; we were well provided for. There were twelve children in my family, nine older than me and two younger. Not all of my siblings lived at home—there were big differences in age between the oldest and youngest, and my four older siblings had already moved out. We only saw them on rare occasions. One was married and the others were at school or living on their own.

I grew up during a time when the relationship between Hutu and Tutsi had worsened, and there was a lot of conflict and discrimination. Sometimes this was really hard to cope with. You did not feel safe or secure, and it would be hard to go to sleep at night wondering if something was going to happen to you. My dad was a good man. He never wanted us to know if we were Tutsi or Hutu. He didn't like that the terms divided people. He would say, "Just know that you are Rwandese, that's it." The rest of society did not think like that, though. Neighbours and other people around you would always know your ethnic identity.

At the beginning of a school year they would ask us to line up by ethnicity: "Tutsi should be here. Hutu should be over there." I didn't like it. I would stay seated and say "I'm just Rwandese," but the other kids and the teachers knew I was Tutsi. They would mock us and call us names. I was bullied, and I didn't look forward to school because of it.

My father would always tell us, "You have to love people whether they're rich, poor, Hutu or Tutsi, or another ethnicity. It doesn't matter. You can dislike the things others do, but you still have to love people and respect them." Those lessons really helped me. I had such trust in my dad that I would always keep those messages in mind and think about what he would want me to do in any given situation. Some days, though, it was very hard to live up to his lessons—because how can you love somebody who doesn't love you? How can you show kindness to someone who hates you and wants to get rid of you? But I would still try.

My dad was a businessman, and when I was around the age of twelve, I would be sent with one of the workers to buy things from the market. The Tutsi women who were working there would call to me, telling me to come and buy from their shops. Instead, I would go around and buy items from both Hutu and Tutsi shops. When I was criticized for doing this I would say, "My dad is a nice guy. He does not have a list of people who I buy from and who I do not." I did not want to buy from people based on ethnicity; instead I tried to follow the lessons my dad had taught me. Later on, it was the Hutu women from the market who ended up saving my life.

APRIL 6, 1994

In 1994 I was thirteen years old and in grade seven, my last year of primary school. I was attending a nearby school and living at home with my family. When the genocide began it wasn't a surprise to anyone. We had known that eventually something was going to happen. The country was controlled by Hutu extremists, and preparations were out in the open. Militia were being trained. It was clear that the government was planning and organizing something.

After the plane crash it took a few days before anything happened in our area. Everything was shut down and no one was able to go to work. We stayed in our home waiting to see what was going to happen. A few days later my cousin, who lived up the street from us, was killed. We knew then that we would be next.

We waited for it to get dark and then went to our neighbour's home. He was Hutu, and we thought that if we hid there we would be safe. He had a big tree with branches that extended across to our side, so we climbed onto the wall that surrounded our home and then onto the tree. There was a lattice that ran down from the tree into the neighbour's yard, so we climbed down and went to hide in his house. Nobody knew how we escaped. The cars were still parked in front of our house, all the doors were locked from the inside, and it looked like we were still at home.

When the killers arrived the next day they were dancing and shouting with excitement; they were convinced we were inside and were about to kill us. They brought a machine to force open the doors and broke into our house. When they got inside and couldn't find us, they became extremely angry. It took them all day to take everything from our home—we could hear them fighting over things, and their frustration at not being able to kill us. They were trying to figure out where we were and how we had escaped. They couldn't believe we had eluded them.

Some of them came over to the house we were hiding in to search for us. The neighbour had barricaded us in a room without a window so that we wouldn't be spotted. The men smashed the windows in his home and looked inside, but they couldn't see anybody. Next they tried to open the door to the room where we were hidden, but for some reason it wouldn't open. God must have been protecting us. They decided they would come back later and remove the door—they were convinced there must be a reason they couldn't open it, that someone had to be hiding inside.

That night our neighbour dug a hole into the side of the room [homes were generally built with clay and dirt, compacted to form walls]. The way he had blocked the door, it couldn't be opened from the inside or the outside. So he created a window in the wall of the room for us to climb out of. That took a long time, and he had to do it very quietly, so that no one would hear what was going on. Sometime around two a.m. we were finally able to climb out of the room. We fled using back lanes, trying to remain hidden, as it was not safe to travel on any main roads or out in the open.

We were close to the hospital, so one of my brothers told us he would go ahead to see if it was safe, and that if we heard him screaming we would know not to come that way. We didn't want him to go. We tried to argue with him; we wanted to stay together and try to find a safe hiding place. But he insisted, and went on ahead of us.

After a minute we could hear his cries as he was killed.

We were overwhelmed with fear, and could do nothing but continue to move and search for somewhere safe to stay. We tried several other places, including a convent and a church, but neither one was accessible. Finally we went to the high school and found people gathered there. They had opened the gates to the school, and the buildings were full of Tutsi who had fled their homes and the killings. We joined the other families and spent what remained of the night there.

Things changed quickly the next day. Around ten a.m. the Interhamwe and local killers arrived and started killing people. I was with my younger sister when the killing began, and we became separated from the rest of the family. Later on I found out that one of my sisters was actually rescued by one of the Interhamwe soldiers who had come to carry out the killings. They had attended school together when they were younger and he recognized her. She was able to bribe him with her jewellery and glasses, and in exchange he took her to a hospital that was being guarded and where she would be safe.

The killing in the school was done exclusively by the men. There were women there as well, but they held the responsibility of walking through the bodies of the victims to retrieve any jewellery, money, extra clothing, or valuable items that had been brought by those fleeing. Before they began killing they ordered everyone to lie down on the floor. Then they took machetes and began to kill.

I am haunted by the sounds of those dying and by the noises the weapons made as they hacked people to death with machetes and beat us with clubs.

For some reason, despite being chopped and cut with a machete, my sister and I didn't die. We were lying with all the dead bodies and were very injured, but by some miracle we were still alive.

Several of the women I used to see at the market had come to the school to help look for items on the bodies. As they were searching, they came near where I was. Despite my disfiguring injuries, the women recognized me. I was still conscious, and I could hear what they were saying: "Oh! That's her! She used to be so kind to us. Why would they kill her?" They realized that I was still alive; they quickly grabbed me and moved me to the side. They told me, "We're so sorry," and then among themselves began discussing what they should do. "We have to do something about her! If we don't do something, she will be gone completely." The killers had plans to return the next day to burn all the bodies. There were so many corpses that they didn't want the work of trying to move and bury them. Burning the bodies would also take care of killing anyone who was still alive.

I knew my sister was also alive, as she had been lying next to me. I had tried to point to her, to indicate that she was alive. When they went to move me again I told them, "Don't take me! My sister is still alive! She is the only one I have left, you have to do something about her too. If you don't, let us die together, because what's the point of surviving without her?"

They replied, "Your sister didn't treat us the same way you treated us." They said they weren't willing to save her.

"Leave us alone then," I said. My sister couldn't stand the women, as they were not very nice people; she had never made any effort to be nice to them. Despite how they acted I had always overlooked it and instead tried to show them kindness and respect. I wanted to obey my dad, to do my best to follow what he had taught me. In return, they had also treated me better. They were not as good or as nice as I was to them, but it was still better than how they acted towards other Tutsi. I told the women again, "Okay. Just leave us alone."

In the end, they decided to help both of us. They said, "Your sister probably won't last long anyway." They were not able to take us anywhere that night, but they moved us to a different area in the school and returned to get us early the next morning before the killers could arrive to dispose of the bodies.

For a short amount of time we were cared for by these same women, but they were very afraid of what their husbands and sons (who were involved in the killings) would do if they were found aiding two Tutsi girls. Soon after rescuing us, they helped us move to the home of two of our Hutu friends. The friends hid us in their home, and cared for our injuries the best they could until we were rescued. I will never forget what both the women and the two friends did for my sister and me. They are the reason we survived. By the end of the same week the RPF began advancing; they were so close to reaching the area that we could hear the guns and fighting going on. There were discussions amongst the killers about finishing off any Tutsi still alive, so that there wouldn't be any survivors or witnesses. We were certain the killers were going to come before the RPF reached us. However, for some reason—maybe how quick the RPF approach was—they ended up leaving us inside the home and fled the area.

When the RPF arrived they rescued my sister and me, carrying us on stretchers to a camp they had set up for survivors. They had created a makeshift medical tent and provided us with some basic care. We stayed there in the RPF camp until the genocide fully ended and we were healed enough to leave. Even though we were both badly injured, both of us survived. Eventually we found out that some of our other siblings had also survived.

One of my sisters had been living in France when the genocide started. She came back to Rwanda to try and find us, fearing that our entire family had been killed. There was no way to contact anyone to see who was alive, as all the infrastructure in the country had been destroyed or damaged. One of my brothers had survived by fleeing to the Congo, and he eventually got hold of her and shared what information he had about the rest of us. My sister, the one who had been helped by the Interhamwe soldier, had survived, along with my other younger sister. Later, when we came to Canada, it was the four of us who had survived the killings at the school that immigrated together, along with one of our cousins.

Once we all finally found one another we tried to return to our home, but we discovered that the house was too damaged to live in and required major repairs. We ended up going to live in the house of an older sister. It was still intact and in okay condition, so we all lived there until we were able to repair the family home.

This sister was married and had two children at the time of the genocide. Her husband and older daughter were both killed, and she was left injured and very close to death. Despite the severity of her condition, she managed to survive and recover from the injuries. Her younger daughter was stabbed in the chest with a knife and had been left for dead. She survived because she had been born with a rare condition that caused her heart to develop on the right side of her body instead of the left, preventing her from dying from the stab wound. A few years after we moved to Canada, the two of them and another cousin also left Rwanda and came to join us.

In total, out of our family of fourteen, only seven of us survived.

Looking back, it is a miracle that I survived with how extensive and serious my injuries were. The medical treatment available was not very good, and there were so many injured people needing help that the resources were very limited. The killers used machetes and wooden clubs, and the pain and suffering as each wound was inflicted was immense. I have been left with permanent scars on my neck, head, and left side from machete wounds.

One injury in particular caused me a lot of problems. I had a deep wound on my head where I had been hacked with the machete. When I was initially given medical treatment they didn't see this wound, as it was covered with my hair and lots of blood. After the genocide it became seriously infected. My head became very swollen, and a large hole formed where the injury was. Eventually it ended up causing me to fall unconscious. I had to be rushed to the hospital, where they had to shave my head and try to wash out and treat the wound. The doctors said it was a miracle that I had survived the injury and also the infection. They didn't understand how I had been able to live with it for so long in that state. It had been extremely painful, but the conditions in the country at that time were exceedingly poor, and accessing treatment was very difficult. It wasn't until I was close to dying from it that I was able to receive medical help. The wound was so large that they were unable to stitch it up; it took a very long time to heal. When I finally recovered, I returned to school and eventually finished high school.

I came to Canada in 2002. We had friends in the United States who would visit us, and they told some Canadian friends about us. That family decided to come and meet us in Rwanda. They were from a small town, and when they visited we invited them to stay with us instead of in a hotel. Over the course of the visit we helped them learn about Rwanda and got to know one another really well. We had a great time with them, and they were grateful for the hospitality we had shown them.

When the family returned to Canada they spoke to their church about us. They shared details about our experiences and explained that, while we were living a decent life, we were suffering from what we had been through and struggling to cope with the ongoing trauma. They asked their church to consider sponsoring us to come to Canada, and the church agreed.

At first we were unsure about the move, and hesitant to accept the offer. It is a hard decision to leave your home and country and everything familiar, and take a risk on the unknown. As difficult as it was to be surrounded with the trauma of Rwanda's past, it was also an intimidating prospect to uproot our lives and begin again in a new and unfamiliar country. We had some family members living in Europe, much closer to Rwanda, so we also considered whether it would be better to try and go there instead. In the end, we decided to accept the opportunity, and the support of the church and the family, and come to Canada.

After we arrived we went to live with the family in their small town. We stayed with them for the first three months. Coming from "the land of a thousand hills," I was shocked to discover how flat Manitoba was. However, the biggest shock was how nice and incredibly kind Manitobans were! I am so glad we decided to host the family back when they came to visit Rwanda, as it was what started the friendship, and eventually what changed our lives for the better. We will always be grateful that Canada opened up its doors to accept us, just as we are thankful for those who opened their doors for us during the genocide.

Initially things were very challenging, as I didn't speak any English other than being able to greet someone. However, people were very nice and understanding, and did their best to help us. We came in April, when it wasn't cold by Canadian standards. We still found it difficult, as for us it was still a lot colder than Rwanda. We arrived at nighttime, and the next day, when we looked outside, we could see the beautiful sunshine. We went to go outside, thinking, "It's going to be so hot out!" Then we opened the door and the cold air hit us. We were like, "No way. This is winter. You have sunshine but it feels cold at the same time?" I will never forget that. It was so new and confusing for us. I didn't understand how it was possible. No matter how much they tell you in advance, you don't get it until you experience it. The language, the cold weather, and the food were the biggest adjustments. Things here didn't taste the same, and at first, we didn't like that. But we got used to it!

The people in the small community were really nice, and really good people. They tried to support and help us. We were coming from a country where basically every person was wounded and suffering from trauma. There was not a good energy, and it was a difficult place to live. So, coming to Canada—seeing people and being in a place without those memories—was so wonderful. It was a very good change for us. Our sponsors actually said, "When we saw you the first time, we saw what you had been through, how much you were suffering, and how traumatized you still were. We had to do something."

We don't take anything for granted about the things we have now, and for the opportunity we had to come to Canada.

When you visit Rwanda now, the energy there is much better, but it is still very difficult. There has been some reconciliation, which has improved things. The first time I went back I thought to myself, "Oh, what have I done?" All the memories returned. Sad things. Horrible things.

For a long time after the genocide I was very angry. I hated people. The violence I lived through is impossible to understand if you haven't experienced it. I wasn't able to forgive, and was consumed by my emotions. I was so depressed and hated my life. I felt that my life had ended with the genocide, and I wanted to commit suicide. It is only through my faith and accepting Jesus in my life that I was finally able to forgive. Finding a way to forgive changes everything.

Now I feel both Canadian and Rwandan, but as time goes by I feel more and more Canadian. I was twenty-two when I moved here, so I have now lived here for most of my adult life. Before I healed I tried to go to university, but I struggled with a lot of issues because of my trauma and couldn't finish. Later, after I had found greater peace through healing and forgiveness, I was able to go back to school. I decided to take courses in aesthetics. It was a much better experience for me, and became the career path I followed.

Several years after moving to Canada, I met my future husband. We met on the exact same month, day of the week, and calendar date that my brother had been killed during the genocide. Prior to this I had difficulties if I even started thinking about the month of April approaching. I would feel traumatized and start remembering things. I had so many horrific experiences attached to the month that it was difficult not to be consumed by these past events every April.

Having a new event that was something positive allowed me to begin having new memories and connections. Every time I think about meeting my husband, I praise the Lord for taking a day that represented trauma and transforming it for me. God allowed that to happen. It changed the meaning of that day for me, the experiences and feelings I had attached to it.

God wanted me to focus on living in the present instead of in the past. I prayed for God to change me, and to change my life, and he did.

[Four]

CoCo

Clotilde, or CoCo, as she goes by, is vibrant and outgoing; she puts her heart into any project she takes on. She volunteers with the local Rwandan community association, helping out at all their events, including the annual commemoration. She's also one of several in the community who participated in a film that documents survivor testimonies from the genocide. That film is shown every year.

Despite how challenging it can be, many survivors share their stories in an effort to raise awareness and help people understand the consequences of breeding hate and discrimination. They feel strongly about the importance of sharing the history of Rwanda and the events that happened there. The goal is to encourage others to practise love and acceptance as well as to stand up and resist attempts at dividing or targeting groups of people.

Survivors like CoCo help to create a supportive network, a community where those who are struggling can seek help from others who've lived through the trauma. In this way they can begin the process of healing. And for those who haven't yet been able to open up and share what they went through, hearing other survivors speak out encourages them to do the same.

CoCo's passion for helping others has also translated into her choice of career. She works with adults with disabilities, and, along with her husband, cares for two live-in clients. It's not hard to see why her clients love her so much: she's a warm, compassionate woman who immediately makes you feel at ease. Despite her difficult past, she's quick to smile and full of energy and excitement.

CoCo's account of her journey to Canada is unique in that it highlights how a single person choosing to help can have a dramatic impact on another's life.

CoCo's Story

I grew up in a happy family. My daddy was a quiet man, and my mom was very outgoing. I was the fifth child, with six siblings— five brothers and one sister. Our family structure was very traditional, with my father working and my mother staying at home and caring for us. Some of my favourite memories are of going to church with my family. My daddy and mom were devoted Christians, and they always spoiled us on Sundays. My father worked very hard to ensure we had everything we could possibly need, and that we had the same kind of items our friends had, such as a TV. We were encouraged to study outside of school, and to work towards getting the highest grades in our class. When we got good grades, Daddy would promise us vacations to places like Kigali to visit our extended family that lived there.

While growing up, it was hard for us to know about the terms "Hutu" and "Tutsi." Our mom and dad wanted to shelter us from the ethnic tensions that existed in the country. They would tell us that if we were asked at school, we were Tutsi, but they didn't explain what it meant. Sometimes in school we were required to stand at different times based on our designated ethnicity. Once we asked our parents about it, and they explained that the terms were based on the number of cows or the size of a person's nose. Still, we didn't really understand what this meant. We had neighbours who were Hutu, and sometimes they would come over to our parties. Our friends at school were both Tutsi and Hutu, and our housemaid was Hutu. These terms meant little to us as young children.

66

My first experience with discrimination involved one of our neighbours, who was Hutu. He didn't want us to pass by his house to get to the main street, and told us we had to find an alternate route. When we asked him why, he tried to intimidate us, saying he didn't want Tutsi near his house. My daddy was such a quiet, kind man, he didn't want to cause any trouble, so he told us that anything someone asked of us, to just do it. He didn't want to explain to us why the neighbour was acting that way. He said that sometimes people are just rude, and that we should just pass in a different way.

I do remember, however, the immense fear that my dad had about parties. He would be so scared that something would happen to one of us. He would tell us that when there was a party we needed to be very careful about who gave us things to eat. We were told to never eat food from a stranger, and to make sure we knew the person, because there could be something in the food. At parties he wanted us to always look around and see who was eating, to make sure it wasn't just us. One time they gave poison to my mom when she was at a party and she got very ill, and my dad was really upset and terrified of it happening again. My mom was very trusting of Hutu people, but for some Hutu they saw this as a way of getting revenge on the Tutsi.

In the year before the genocide I became more aware that I was Tutsi. At school, there were times when they would have us perform skits where we had to act out that we were attending a Tutsi funeral. We would tell our parents about this when we came home from school. During this time one of my aunts was working on the Tutsi side of the government. She would have news about what was going on in the country and government and would share this information with my mom. Mom would want to talk about these things with Dad, but he didn't want to be a part of politics; he just wanted peace. He wanted a quiet life and no issues with the neighbours. My dad was very scared by the information my aunt was sharing with my mom. He would tell her that she needed to be careful about what her sister told her, because my aunt was a Tutsi and was working in the government, which made her a target. If something were to happen, Mom would also become a target and would be killed because of her sister.

When I think back to my childhood, I realize that my parents were living in such a hard situation, as they were Tutsi and knew everything that was going on in the country. We were so young and they tried to protect us. My mom and dad tried their best to make us happy, and to provide us with anything we wanted or needed. Maybe our parents knew something was going to happen leading up to the genocide. But as kids, we had no idea.

APRIL 6, 1994

It was a Wednesday night when the plane was shot down. I was eleven years old at the time. The next morning my mom came and woke my sister and me at seven a.m., telling us that the president had been killed. This was different from our normal routine of rising at seven-thirty, and we were not eager to get out of bed. I didn't really understand the significance of what she was telling us; I thought it was nothing. However, she insisted that it was really important, and that we needed to get up immediately.

Once we were dressed, my parents tried their best to explain what was going on. My dad insisted that we eat breakfast before going anywhere. His biggest concern was that we would suffer or die from hunger, and he wanted to make sure that did not happen to any of his children. He gave each one of us money, so that no matter what happened to the others, we would each have a way to get food and water. His concern was not for his own well-being, but rather for the survival of his children.

My mom wanted to divide us up so that there would be a better chance of someone in our family surviving. I went with one brother and one sister to see an aunt who lived a twenty-five-minute walk away. She had moved to the city recently and wasn't well known, so my mom thought we would be safer there. My six-year-old brother stayed with my mom, and my other brother escaped and hid with a Hutu family. My eldest brother had been away at school but was home for Easter holidays. He survived by hiding elsewhere, and also because many people did not recognize him and thought he was Hutu.

Before we left I asked my mom if we would come back that night. She said maybe, but that we needed to just go and see what would happen. My dad did not want to leave; he wanted to stay at the house. He was feeling ill, and kept telling us he loved us. Despite our pleas for him to come with us, he refused. My mom insisted on staying with him. When we left we still had the belief that our parents would come and join us later. I still did not really understand what was going on.

Our location did not remain a secret for long. Our housekeeper, who was Hutu, told our neighbours where we had been sent. That evening, one of our neighbours came to my aunt's house to tell us that he had killed my father and that we would be next. My daddy had been killed only hours after we left that morning. The neighbour had come to intimidate us, to see our reaction. He told us that they could come and kill us at any time. In the early stages of the genocide, the first priority was to kill the men, and then kill the rest of the family later.

Despite these threats, we remained with my aunt but went into hiding. She was a member of the Presbyterian church, and she lived inside the church compound. It provided a greater level of protection, as the killers were reluctant to enter inside. The pastor, who was a Hutu, did not want anyone killed; he tried to hide those on the compound, and would sometimes cook and bring us food, sometimes water. On occasion they would allow us to go back to get what we had in my aunt's house, and they would cook that food for us. We were too scared and panicky to do very much. Some days we had no food, but whatever we got one day my aunt would divide up so that we would also have food the next day.

The killers would often come looking for us, but remained fearful of attacking the compound. They would knock on the doors, or try to force them open. They would loot the buildings and take everything they could find. Sometimes the killers would send a letter to threaten to come back and kill everyone.

At the compound they would move us to different rooms to try and keep us safe. Once, the killers came and found the room we were hiding in, but were unable to get the door open. They told us that we must come out on the count of three or they would throw a grenade inside and kill us all. We knew that if we came out we would be killed by machete. My aunt told us not to be scared, as it would be better to be killed by a grenade than a machete. Another time we were put in a room with my aunt, her five kids, and many other Tutsi. There was nowhere to use the washroom and people had to go wherever they were standing. We stayed jammed in that room for long periods, and were then moved to another room. It was very traumatizing. We didn't really understand what was going on, just that we were struggling because of who we were.

Despite the efforts of the pastor, it eventually became too difficult to continue to protect us. The killers started to threaten his life, saying that if he stopped them and continued to hide Tutsi, he would die. He warned us, coming to tell my aunt he had received a letter from the killers stating that they were coming the next day to kill the Tutsi and that nothing would stop them. He told everyone who had somewhere else to go to be prepared to leave. My aunt decided that since my brother and I looked Hutu, we should leave and try to hide somewhere else. She sent us with one of our cousins to our uncle's house to see if we could survive.

I reached my uncle's house with my brother and my cousin. My uncle, his wife, and their three youngest children were still alive. Their other three children had been away at school when the violence broke out, so they did not know if they were dead or somehow still alive.

My aunt stayed with four of her sons. Just after we left, they came and killed her. She was holding her youngest son in her arms as she was slaughtered.

My sister, who was still at the compound, saw this happen. One of the Hutu among the killers knew my father and recognized her. He said that our father was a good man, and offered to take her and help hide her. He told the others that she was a Hutu and had ended up there by mistake. She later escaped and joined us at my uncle's house.

During the five days we spent at my uncle's house, the killers would come and threaten to kill us. At night we often hid outside the home in case they came. During the day killing was less common, as many people were still living normal lives, so we were safer. Mom was still alive and had found our location, so she would come and visit us in the evenings. She had my youngest brother, the six-year-old, still with her. When she visited we would beg and cry to go with her, and she would explain to us that we couldn't. She was hiding in the house of someone who used to work with my dad, but she was not allowed to bring anyone else with her because the family was scared of being discovered hiding Tutsi.

After the fifth day, the killers came at night and took my uncle and his wife. They told us that they were coming back to get us. We fled, taking my three young cousins with us, and tried to go to the place where my mom was in hiding. My mom was distraught: first her husband had been killed, and then her sister, and now her brother was dead as well. Every place she thought to be safe turned out not to be. She said that the killers should be called so that her children would not suffer any longer, and we could at least all die together.

We were lucky to find out that my oldest brother (the one who had been away at school) was in the city and was still alive. He came to see our mother and found us there. He was twenty-two. He knew our dad had been killed, and that my mom was too distraught to care for us. He tried to find a way to hide us. Our house at that point was still intact and still had our stuff in it, so there was the potential that we could try and sell things, and then pay someone to assist us. It is important to remember that

71

during the genocide, some of the Hutu in Rwanda tried to help the Tutsi. However, they were also traumatized and threatened. Many would eventually tell Tutsi to leave because their own life was being threatened for hiding us.

Eventually, my brother found a family that was willing to help us. The wife was a Tutsi and the husband a Hutu, and they had plans to escape to the Congo. He said he and his brother would help hide us for a few days and then arrange to help us get to the Congo. His wife was in hiding too. My brother also found a Hutu schoolmate who agreed to take my sister to the Congo.

We split up in order to escape. I was with my brother as well as the young son of one of the men who was helping us. The man hiding us went and bought us white T-shirts and blue pants so that we would appear as if we were wearing school uniforms and studying in the Congo. He also taught us some Congolese words so that we could answer questions in Swahili and explain that we were going to school.

When we got to the Congo, we met a Tutsi woman who had escaped and was helping survivors at the border. She must have known my mother, because when she saw me she said my mother's name, saying that I looked like her. I told her that yes, that was my mother, and she let us stay with her until the next day. She knew of an orphanage that had been located in Rwanda but had moved to the Congo when the conflict broke out. She felt that we could go and stay there. At the time we didn't know what an orphanage was—we thought it was for kids whose families were rude and mean.

When we arrived at the orphanage they agreed to let us stay there, and said they would provide us with food and water. If our family came we would be able to go, but they would keep us safe until that time. They knew what was going on in Rwanda; they had kids already there who were traumatized by the genocide.

When we left Rwanda, my older brother stayed behind to try and help Mom escape. The killers were searching for her and her son, who could be identified because he wore glasses. My brother evaded them by removing his glasses; without them, no one could clearly tell if he was Hutu or Tutsi. He took my six-year-old brother and hid in different places.

He saw the people who took my mom. He had hoped that by staying behind he could help her. He asked the family she was hiding with if they could assist in selling our family house in order to protect her, but he was told that the Hutu would just wait and take anything that was left if we all died.

My mom was killed on June 21, 1994.

After this, my brother came to the Congo. He found a place near the orphanage to stay. Eventually we discovered that two of our other siblings (my sister and one of my other brothers) had also successfully escaped and made it to the Congo.

Sometime after July 14th, we left the Congo to return to Rwanda. We waited until the RPF had taken control of the country and it was safe for us to return. Of my family of nine, six of us survived the genocide. We lost my parents and one of my brothers, as well as most of our extended family.

We went back to our old house, but it was a mess: the doors were gone, and there was blood on the walls. All the materials and furniture were gone too, but the house was still there. It was very hard for us, as we were so traumatized. One of my relatives who survived offered to put us in different families, but my brother said no, he didn't want us separated into different houses; he wanted us to stay together as a family.

We tried to repair the house. In the beginning, we kept thinking of where our mom and dad used to sleep. It was very difficult; no one wanted to enter my parents' room. My brother tried to do what he could to change the house, but his funds were very limited and he was still going to school. He said that we needed to return to school as well, but we struggled with fears about what was coming. He tried to fill the role of our parents despite his age and lack of income. He reminded us that as long as we survived we should continue to try our best.

After a few years he made the decision to get married. We were all very shocked. He decided to give us time to let us process it, to be able to handle the change. When I finished high school, I said I wanted to go to university and work at the same time to help care for my siblings. He was worried that we wouldn't be able to handle it, but we wanted to free him from his responsibilities so that he could start a new family and not have to care for us.

In 2005 I was working in a hotel at Lake Kivu, where one of the guests was an American woman. She asked my colleague about the species of a bird that flew by, but my coworker didn't know, so I told her the name of it. She was surprised and asked how I knew English. I told her I had learned it from working at the hotel, from being at the front desk and a secretary.

We got to know one another better during her stay. She came to visit, and met my siblings. I explained to her what had happened to my parents; prior to that, she did not know about the genocide. She asked if I would come and visit her in the U.S., saying that I would become like her daughter; every April she would see if I could visit her so that I wouldn't be alone. I asked if she thought it was actually possible. She was a journalist and said she could apply for a visa for me to come and visit. She did apply, and the U.S. Embassy called me to do an interview. At the time I was like, "Wow, how can this kind of thing happen?" Sometimes she also helped us out financially, as at that time my brother was married and my sister was in university, so I was fully responsible for supporting the family.

I visited her in the U.S. in April of 2007. She could see how I struggled with the trauma of still living in Rwanda after everything that had happened. She treated me as her own child, and cared about my well-being. She suggested I look at immigrating to North America. She wanted me to come and live in the U.S. but didn't think I would be able to due to the tough restrictions, so she suggested

I look into Canada. She said if my story is real, then I would be accepted. To this day I view her as my mother and visit her, talk with her, and send her flowers on Mother's Day.

I came in March 2008. It was snowing, and I didn't know anyone here in Canada. I came through Montreal; I had on open shoes and wasn't even wearing a jacket. When the people at Immigration saw me they asked how nobody had warned me about the weather. The place I had visited in the u.s. was not cold, and while the woman had tried to give me a jacket, she had forgotten to warn me about my shoes.

Even though life in Rwanda had been so hard because of the trauma, when I first got to Canada I wished I could just go back to my country. Everything was new and challenging. I was lucky to meet some Rwandan friends soon after moving who assisted me with adjusting to the changes.

The first big change was the weather. When it is raining in Rwanda, people stay inside and things are closed, but here in Canada, even when it snows people go out, and things are open. My new friends told me that I could not wait for the snow to stop to do things, or I'd be waiting three or four months, since this is Canada. I had to go and buy a jacket and boots. Even though the weather was bad, people were so nice, and tried to help me adjust.

When I'd go to church events I would see how nice people are, how they were excited and happy to see me, and how they wanted to know about me and my experiences. When I shared my story, they would reassure me that now I was here in Canada and was safe. I also went to ESL school, and everyone was willing to help me learn English. I felt comforted, and welcomed. In April especially, they would send me flowers and help me get through the difficult months.

Another change I had to make was learning how to cook in Canada. I had never used a microwave or stove before, so had to learn how they worked and how to use them to prepare meals.

One of the first foods I ate in Canada was actually pizza. I was so excited to see it! Now I have eaten it so much that I'm tired of it. When I first came here I didn't even know I could buy beans and rice. I didn't even know there was grass and trees, because in the movies when they show Canada they only show cities, so that is what I imagined.

One of my favourite memories was from my first job. I was living in London, Ontario, and found a job working at Mac's convenience store. At the end of the month they gave me my paycheque for $800, and I thought that was a lot of money; I was putting the money into Rwandan currency and thinking I was quite rich. I felt this way until I went to the store to buy groceries. That's when I realized how expensive the prices are for everything compared to Rwanda. In Rwanda, if you spent $20 on potatoes it would last you for months, and here things don't last that long and cost so much more. But I still remember the excitement I felt about that first paycheque.

People in Canada were so nice; they were friendly, and would teach me things. The beginning was very difficult because everything was new, but in the end it was okay because people were so welcoming and willing to help.

I have since been back to Rwanda several times, for my wedding, my sisters' wedding, and to visit family. I started dating my husband while I was still in Rwanda. He was living in the U.K. at the time, but we had been introduced through family members. Once I became a permanent resident here in Canada (and after we were married), I applied for him to join me, and he moved here in 2011.

It is very hard now for people to come to Canada. My siblings want to come visit, but it's hard even to get a tourist visa for them. So, for now, it is easiest for us to go there when we want to see them. They are all working now; my oldest brother has four kids, and my sister is married with two kids.

I feel more Canadian now than I do Rwandan. Sometimes when I go home and people say they are coming at two p.m., I expect them to come at two p.m. Here when I say dinner is at six p.m., I start to put the food out at six p.m. I am used to everything being punctual and on time now. Even hospitality works differently: here, if you go visit someone you may bring something with you, like drinks, but when I do that in Rwanda I have to explain that in Canada that's how we do it, whereas there you would just go to someone's house and it would be their responsibility to host you. Even something as simple as sneezing in a tissue versus just using a hand is different. When my husband and I visit Rwanda now we try to teach them how things are done in Canada, how they are different.

Last December when I was in Rwanda, we had a housemaid helping. We didn't want to cook, as we had visitors constantly coming to the house. We ended up in the kitchen helping, and the housemaid said that we don't act like Rwandans anymore. She would also ask, "How come your husband is helping in the kitchen?" It was a good experience.

The more time we spend in Canada and the more experiences we have, the more I like it. Here people are very open and expressive, and we are learning that; back home, people are very closed off, and not as open. Here if you don't do your work, no one will do it for you. Canadians are more organized, and get things finished.

We work with people with disabilities, and have two roommates we support. One we've had since 2013, when we first bought the house, and our second roommate moved in last summer. We get feedback from the doctors and supervisors, and from the people we are supporting, so we strive to do a good job. When we were going away on vacation we had to put together a small book for one of our roommates explaining to him that we would be coming back, because he thought we were leaving him. We were gone one month, and now he doesn't want us to go again. It meant a lot to us that he felt that good about living here.

[Five]

Annick

I've spent the last ten years studying the Rwandan genocide and meeting with survivors to hear their testimonies. When you become involved in this kind of work, you learn to build a barrier—to distance yourself from the stories so that you don't become traumatized in turn. It doesn't mean that you aren't affected by them or that you lack empathy; instead, it's a protective mechanism so that you don't get pulled in too deeply and become unable to cope with the things you're being told.

When I set up the interview with Annick, I'd already finished recording some of the interviews for this book and felt I was doing well at maintaining such distance and managing my emotions. I was connected with her through CoCo, who'd told me that Annick was passionate about sharing her story and helping others, and would want to take part. I didn't anticipate the profound impact Annick's survivor testimony would have on me, and the challenges I'd face in documenting and working on it. After our first meeting, I would be haunted by her story for weeks to come.

Annick is close to me in age, and so with each time marker she cited I found myself reflecting on where I'd been during my own life. Annick grew up near Nyamata; her family was killed at the church there. When I listen to survivor testimonies I usually have a difficult time putting the locations together, given that I'm somewhat geographically challenged. In this case, though, it was different. In 2009, Nyamata was the first memorial I visited in Rwanda. I'd returned three times since, having had my most recent visit shortly before the interview. And so as Annick told her story my mind followed the places she talked about like a movie reel filling in the landscape and the scenery. I had chills when she described having her arm grabbed at the church gate, the very gate where I'd stood less than a month before.

Annick's strength and courage are apparent in the way she speaks and in the presence she has. Although parts of her journey may be difficult to relate to here in Canada, her story also contains elements shared by anyone who has lived through trauma. Annick is an inspiration for others who face similar challenges with their mental health, who struggle to find their way in life. Her testimony shows that healing and finding a purpose after trauma is possible. She is gentle, compassionate, and caring, but also confident— not with the kind of confidence gained by success or fuelled by arrogance, but an inner confidence that comes from having struggled and survived.

In 2017 Annick returned to Rwanda to explore opportunities for supporting those who are still trapped by the horrors they lived through. She's passionate about using her journey of faith and healing to help others who are coping with trauma.

Annick's Story

I grew up in a Christian family, the ninth-born of ten kids, with four brothers and five sisters. My dad was a pastor with the Anglican church and my mom stayed home and cared for us. Life was beautiful as a child; I was happy and surrounded by love. As the last girl with older parents, I was very well loved and cared for. I can't tell you exactly when I realized I was a Tutsi; I just always knew. I can also remember my dad talking about how the Hutu hated us. I never understood why. I just knew that they hated us, and I was always scared by that.

We lived in an area known as Nyamata, where there was a large population of Tutsi. My dad used to teach history, so between his knowledge and his own experiences while growing up, he knew a lot about Rwanda. He was so knowledgeable that people used to come to our house to interview him. From my father, I learned that Tutsi had been forced to move to the area, and that this had been done intentionally, to make it harder for them to survive. They had been pushed from their homes and well-developed areas to Nyamata, where at the time nothing existed. Some of the families we knew had fled from places like Ruhengeri, where killings and attacks had happened.

My favourite moments were when my siblings were on vacation from school. Most of my childhood they were away at boarding schools, so holidays like Christmas were really special times. Sometimes we had twenty or twenty-five people in our home, as cousins would come to join us. My daddy also had a lot of friends, and every few months we hosted parties that were a lot of fun. When I close my eyes I can still picture those parties—friends and their kids coming over, having drinks and food to celebrate, everyone filled with happiness.

In 1989 my second oldest brother left home to go to university in Uganda. Then, when the civil war broke out in 1990, he went to fight with the RPF. He died soon after. I did not learn of his death until after the genocide. Nobody told me he had died, so for a long time I believed he was still living in Uganda and that I would see him again.

My dad was very supportive of the RPF; he would sometimes travel to their fundraising events before the start of the civil war. I suspect that the government knew this, and that when the genocide began he was near the top of the list to be killed. In the years following the RPF invasion, soldiers and Hutu neighbours would come to our house and conduct searches. They would break stuff, slash the mattresses, and intimidate us. They didn't have confirmation that my brother had been a soldier, but they suspected it. They would regularly visit all the Tutsi families in the area and ask them where any missing sons and daughters were.

In 1992, when I was ten years old, I remember that they started killing Tutsi in the Bugesera region. They began burning down houses, and people started fleeing and coming to the churches. We were living close to the church where my dad was a pastor, so people were also coming to our house and to the local school. At the time, I was not scared by what was going on because I did not see anyone dying. People who were older were scared, but I really had no feelings of fear. Some of my friends from school were sleeping in the church and in the school. We had no classes, so I would get to go and play with them.

During this time, it also became common in school for the teachers to ask us to stand up so that they could count the number of Tutsi in the class. The days the counting would occur, there would be tension in the room between the students. I had one close friend named Yvonne who was Hutu, but after they started counting us in class, we no longer talked. It seemed that even the Hutu kids did not like us Tutsi. I went home the first time it happened and asked my father why they were doing this. He didn't explain it to me, but just said that every time they called for Tutsi I should be the first student to stand up. Dad felt I should be proud of who I was, and should not be afraid.

Despite being only kids, when we walked on the roads near our house people would shout at us and call us names, like "cockroaches." Even though our school was close by, Dad always had an older sibling come and meet me and my little brother to walk us home because he feared for our safety. My parents also brought home all my siblings who had been attending boarding schools, and instead sent them to attend schools close to home.

In 1993 my dad retired from his job as a pastor. We moved into a house in Kayumba, where we lived until the genocide began.

When the genocide occurred, I was twelve years old. The night of the plane crash I was at my cousin's house for a sleepover. First thing the next morning, April 7th, my dad sent my brother over to get me. I knew something was wrong when he arrived and told me that we needed to hurry home, that the president had died. I did not know what was going to happen or what to expect, but I did know that the president was a bad person who hated Tutsi.

My whole family was home except for three of my siblings. My one brother had already been killed in the war (which I hadn't been told) and my oldest brother had fled the country in 1993. He had been hunted and intimidated by soldiers, and they had threatened to kill him. He went to live in Kenya, and stayed there, working with the RPF. One of my older sisters was also away; it was Easter vacation, and she had gone to Kigali to visit some other cousins.

When I got home my house was full of people—all my aunts, uncles, and their kids. Most Rwandans at this time had big families, with anywhere from seven to twelve kids. So you can imagine what our home looked like with five or six families gathered there. I went to my mom to ask her what was going on and why all the people were there. She took me into the bedroom and told me to put on extra clothes in layers. When I asked her why, she replied that we had to flee from the house, that we were going to go to the church. I remembered that two years earlier something similar had happened: we went to the church to greet everyone who was arriving; they were sleeping at the church, and it was a lot like camping. I felt excited that we were going to do the same, and that now it was my turn to have a fun adventure.

The excitement did not last long. That same day, my three brothers and my male cousins left the house to see what was going on in the neighbourhood. We could see houses burning on the surrounding hills. I still wasn't scared, but any feelings of fun or excitement had worn off. When my brothers arrived home, they told my dad that he needed to leave the house because he was on the list of people to be killed that day. Dad left to go hide with another Tutsi friend.

That night we all slept outside in the bushes. My father joined us in our hiding place. Nobody was talking; there was just silence. I could hear people screaming on the other hills, and see the fear of those older than me. My aunt was unable to stay still, and was pacing back and forth in distress. My brothers were somehow still getting information, and found out that two of my father's best friends had been killed.

The next morning we returned to the house, leaving my father behind, hidden in the bushes. My mom and my aunts cooked enough food to feed everyone, and then we returned to the bushes. On April 9th the Interhamwe came closer to where we were. My dad said it was not safe for all of us to stay in the bushes, that the best plan was to try and go to the church or the commune office. He said he would stay in hiding, but that the rest of the family should go. My father was born in 1938 and was getting older; he was in his late fifties. He told my mom's brother that he could not afford to run and be hunted by people he knew. I think he wanted to maintain his dignity, and did not want to spend the last bit of his life running and fleeing from those he used to employ and help provide for.

That was the last time I saw my dad. The image is imprinted in my mind. We had been hiding on a hill, and as we walked down I looked back and could see him standing there at the top, all alone. I had no idea that this was to be my fnal memory of him.

We travelled down from the hills on our way towards the Nyamata church. We passed people who had been hacked by machetes and were not dead yet. Some were running, and bleeding everywhere. When we got to the town of Nyamata we could see the bodies of people lying in the streets. We began running towards the church, and the closer we got, the more bodies there seemed to be. People were screaming and shouting and babies were crying. My mom told us to grab the hand of another person so that we would be in groups of two. The Interhamwe was getting close, and started shooting at everyone who was running. My sister and I were holding hands, and we lost sight of the rest of our family. We spotted a house and ran inside. The guy in the house was a Hutu and his wife was a Tutsi. There were many other people hiding there, and kids we had gone to school with were hiding under the beds.

Within fifteen minutes the Interhamwe burst into the house and demanded that everyone come out of hiding and gather in the living room. I can't explain how I felt at that moment. I was terrified, standing there in front of men holding machetes covered in blood. You know you are going to be killed. They are killing those around you, and you know you are next.

Every time people ask me how I survived, I say it was a miracle. Every day was the day you were going to die. If you made it to the next day, it was only because of a miracle. There in the house was the first time I faced death up close. I could see the faces of those who didn't look human. They were ugly, angry, and hungry to kill you.

Most of the people in the house were kids my age or my sister's [sixteen]. One of the soldiers decided that they shouldn't bother killing us at that moment. He told the others, "Just leave them. Let them go to where the others are. They can go to the CND." [During the temporary ceasefire brought by the 1993 Arusha Peace Accords, the RPF had been able to station six hundred soldiers inside Kigali at the Centre Nationale de Developpement, known as the CND. When the genocide began, this became a sarcastic term the Interhamwe used to describe the locations where Tutsi had been rounded up in large groups.]

We were sent to the area where others were gathered and being guarded by the Interhamwe. We saw my uncle, and sat with him and some of his children. He told us our mom was there but that it would be impossible to reach her—by this point so many people had been gathered in the area that it looked like a crowd in a stadium. Everyone was scattered and split up and we couldn't see any of our other siblings.

We had been there for less than twenty minutes when we saw buses pull up and park. After that everything happened very, very quickly. Interhamwe piled out of the buses wielding machetes and other weapons and began attacking everyone who was gathered.

We stood up and started running.

Someone ran between my sister and me, forcing us apart. I could see her running; she yelled at me to keep going. After a few minutes I lost sight of her in the crowd.

My dad's words came back to me—he had told us to go to the church—so I continued running in that direction.

When I got to the church gate, someone grabbed me. It was a woman named Grace, the wife of one of my dad's friends. She seized my hand and told me that I couldn't enter the church. I tried to resist her but she wouldn't relent. I wanted to go in, as I was certain that was where I would find my family. She continued to tell me I couldn't, and asked that I follow her.

Grace's four daughters were with her, and she took us to hide in a banana plantation. We stayed there for the night. I was restless and wanted to go back and search for my family. Grace kept reassuring me; she told me not to worry, and that we would meet up with my family later. I think at this point everyone still thought the events that were happening were temporary. There was a belief that things would calm back down and the killings and violence would come to an end.

The next day we continued to hide at the plantation. The Interhamwe had resumed killing people in the area, and more Tutsi were arriving to hide. Grace's daughters, who were older than me, would take me a short distance away to talk and distract me while Grace asked the newcomers questions. She tried to find out where they were coming from and what was happening at the church. I wanted to know what was going on, but she did her best to shield me from any news.

Near Nyamata there is a bridge that runs over the Nyabarongo, where they were throwing people who were still alive, as well as dead bodies, into the river. Most Rwandans did not know how to swim. Near the banks of the river were very high grasses and a swampy area where no one goes because it is so dirty. We left the plantation and went to hide in these grasses. Most of the Tutsi who survived the attacks in the Nyamata region did so by hiding there.

I eventually lost track of the days and what was happening. We would sleep at one place for two or three days, and then move to the next spot. I no longer knew where we were, just that we were living in the bushes and had nothing to eat. Throughout this time I continued to ask Grace, "Where is my family? When are we going to go back?"

She just kept telling me, "Don't worry, we will go back," or, "Everyone is coming, we are going to meet them," in an effort to reassure me and keep me calm.

We saw lots of other Tutsi also in hiding, attempting to flee the killings. There were six of us in my group—myself, Grace, and her four daughters—but we often hid with other people at night, splitting up again in the morning. If we saw the same ones the next night we would hear about different people who had been killed that day. We lived this way, in a constant state of fear, day after day.

Sometimes we would find raw food like cassava or sweet potatoes to eat. The adults would go during the night to any nearby plantations and dig in search of anything edible. Some days they were successful and we had food, but on many days we were very hungry.

I can remember one day when we were extremely thirsty and unable to search for water because the killing going on around us was so intense. We were trapped—hiding in the bushes in the same spot for two or three days. It had rained, so we survived by licking raindrops off the leaves of the trees.

Despite frequently moving, we were still in the area near the river and eventually reached a point where it was necessary to cross the river to get to the province, Gitarama, on the other side. Grace thought it would be safer there, and that the killings may not have started yet.

The Interhamwe were waiting in the area for people to come and try cross the river so that they could kill them. There were also

Hutu with small boats offering transportation for those who could pay. At the time, we thought those Hutu were saving people's lives. We found out later that they were really just using the situation as an opportunity to make money, while knowing that those they transported would just be killed on the other side.

Grace paid money for one of these boats for us to cross the river, thinking we would be safer. As we crossed the river, I remember watching people commit suicide by jumping in the water. They were intentionally drowning themselves so that they would not be killed by machete. One woman first threw each of her kids in the river, and then jumped in herself to die.

Somehow, we survived the trip across the water and away from the river. We travelled to a nearby church and slept there for a few days, until people arrived to begin killing.

Next we travelled to a second church where they hadn't started killing yet. The same situation repeated itself: we stayed for a few days, and then the killers arrived there too.

All this time we were travelling by foot, walking and hiding in the bushes. Grace began saying that we needed to find a way to walk to Burundi, that it would be our only chance of surviving.

We had been travelling in the direction of Butare, approximately a hundred kilometres southwest of Nyamata, and eventually reached the city. I remembered that one of my older sisters used to come to Butare on vacation to visit a cousin and her family who lived there. I told Grace about this, and being a close family friend, she had heard about this cousin as well.

When we arrived, my cousin and her family were shocked to see us. They had been receiving information about what was occurring in Kigali and didn't know if anyone was still alive. My cousin wanted to know how I had managed to get there, and how I even knew she lived in Butare. She was living in a compound of the company she worked for, and the director of the company came to the house to greet us. I found out later that he was a Hutu extremist, but at the time I thought it was a sign of what close friends he was with my cousin and her family. Under the guise of being supportive, he asked us what had happened to our family and how we had made it there. I believed my family was alive and safe in the church at Nyamata, so I just told him they were still back home. Later on, this same man came to look for me to kill me.

We thought we were now safe and had escaped the killings. Things were still normal where my cousin lived; they were still in their house, and everything seemed good. We all took showers for the first time in weeks, slept in a house, and ate cooked food.

Grace told my cousin and her husband about what we had travelled through and what had occurred in Nyamata. She tried to convince them that it wasn't safe to stay in Butare, and that we needed to continue on to Burundi. My cousin and her husband didn't believe that the killings would reach as far as Butare. They told her that it would be safe to stay here. Grace insisted that she and her daughters needed to resume their journey, and asked if she could take me with her to Burundi. My cousin turned her down and again insisted that it would be best for me to stay because everything would be fine.

One week after we arrived in Butare, they started killing in the area. We began hiding and sleeping in the bushes every night. During one of the attacks, when we were running through the bushes in the dark, I lost contact with my cousin and her kids and found myself alone. I became very angry, wondering why we had not left with the others; I thought about how they were probably safe in Burundi while I was fleeing from killers. Eventually I found another girl who had been living at my cousin's house, and we hid together.

Everything became extremely difficult. We had nothing to eat, nowhere to go, and no idea where my cousin and her family were. I kept thinking about my family back in Nyamata, and tried to figure out if there was a way to get back to them. I questioned why I had not fought harder against Grace and gone to join them in the church. Why had I believed and listened to her?

At this point, I had no idea that my entire family had been killed. I was thinking of the events in 1992, where everyone had gathered in the church for safety and all of them had survived. I was convinced that my family was still alive and wondering where I was.

"A month has gone by and they don't know where I am, and the people here, they are going to kill me," I would think to myself.

Eventually I decided that the best idea would be to find the director who my cousin worked for. I remembered his name and how he had come to the house to greet us, and I thought he would be willing to hide me. I left my hiding place and found someone to give me directions to his home. When I arrived, he asked me what I was doing there. I explained that I needed a place to stay and asked if I could stay with him. I was shocked when he said no. I thought he was a good friend of my cousin's family, and I couldn't understand why he would turn me away. His home was located within the same company compound as my cousin's.

He told me again in a much angrier voice, "You can't stay here, and I don't want you in this neighbourhood!" He said he would be sending people to kill me, and that if they didn't kill me, he'd come and kill me himself.

I left his house but I was very hungry and thirsty. The maid at the house waved me over; she told me to hide nearby, and that she would bring me something. I don't know if she was Hutu or Tutsi, but she brought me some food and some milk. Because I was so hungry from days without food, I was only able to eat a small amount without getting sick. After that I returned to the bushes where I had been hiding. I was crying, and feeling desperate. The other girl I had been hiding with was gone, so I was now entirely alone.

I stayed there in the bush for some time, but I started feeling really, really tired. I didn't think I could keep going and continue to hide. It was raining, and I could see Hutu working in the fields nearby. I decided to go and talk to them, and ask them to either hide me or kill me, whatever they chose to do. I went to them, and one of them agreed to hide me for the night. He told me to stay hidden in the bushes until it was dark, and that he would whistle when he returned for me.

When he came back he took me to his house outside the compound in the village. They were extremely poor; it was the first time I had seen real poverty of that degree. It was not that my family was rich, but this was a much greater level of poverty than I had experienced before. They did not have plates for eating, and were using banana leaves for their food. I stayed there for the night, but the next morning his brother, who was the leader of the Interhamwe in the area, came to the house. His brother had heard that a Tutsi was there. He told the man who had helped me that he had to kill me, or he would kill me himself. The man reassured his brother. He told him not to waste his time, that he would kill me later.

His brother told him, "I trust you will kill her," and left.

When he was gone the man turned to me and said, "I am not going to kill you, but I am also not going to keep you, so you have to leave."

I left the house unsure of what to do next. There was an elderly couple working in the field, so I went to them to ask if they could help me. They told me they were the parents of the man I had just stayed with and the Interhamwe leader, and that they had heard about me. They demanded I leave the field and stay away from their property.

I started to feel hopeless again. I had no idea where to go; I was in a place that was completely unfamiliar to me. I walked aimlessly all day, making no effort to hide. I wanted to die, because I didn't know what to do or how to continue to survive. I was tired, and eventually sat down next to a pathway.

Two women saw me sitting there; they came to ask what I was doing and why I was in their field. I attempted to lie about who I was, claiming, "I am not a Tutsi, I just came to visit my cousin who is a maid." I then explained that the family she was working for had fled.

They looked at me and said, "Oh, you're a Hutu?" I claimed that I was. Despite my Tutsi appearance, my nose was not really like a

Tutsi nose, so I told them that I was mixed; my mom was a Tutsi but passed when I was young, and my dad was a Hutu. In Rwanda your ethnicity was based upon your father.

I offered to work for them, despite the fact that the women were clearly very poor. They had been on their way to fetch water, and told me to stay where I was until they returned. While I was waiting for them the girl from my cousin's house somehow found me, and she joined me by the path. When the women returned they took us to their house. I told them that the other girl was the cousin I had come to visit.

The family was very cruel and emotionally abusive. They would constantly tell me that they knew I was a Tutsi based on how I walked, my long fingers, and my features. They would often ask me to do things I was not capable of because of my age and size. I would be asked to lift things that were too heavy for me to carry, and sent to fetch water with huge jerry cans or to work in the field. Sometimes they would tell me to leave the house because I couldn't do the work they wanted done. When this happened I would sit outside near the house, not knowing what else to do, until they would eventually call me back for more work.

It had been two months since the genocide had begun and I had left my home. In my heart, I felt that this was what my future now looked like: working and living in this kind of situation.

The other girl did not stay at the same house as me and was sent to work for some relatives of the two women. She was sixteen years old at the most, and went through a similar experience. We would meet when we were sent to fetch water. They would intentionally send us on tasks where we would be out in the open so that if anyone wanted to kill us, they could.

When the local Interhamwe would return from killings they would stop for a rest and to drink and eat. I would try to hide if I saw them coming. If the family noticed me doing this they would force me to serve drinks to the killers. The men would taunt me, telling me that they were saving me for last, and would discuss the various people they had killed that day and how they had killed them. They would wipe their machetes off on the grass and then go home drunk, only to go out killing the next day.

The one thing that gave me hope was that the family frequently listened to the radio and I was able to hear news that the RPF was advancing. I didn't understand or know much about what was happening in the country, but I did know that if the RPF arrived I would be safe because they were Tutsi. I started to believe that they would come, and that at some point I would be free of the family.

One day when we were out fetching water, we heard someone calling our names. We went to see who it was—and hiding in the bush was my cousin's husband. He told us that he was being hunted but hadn't been found yet, and asked us where we were staying. We gave him the names of the people we were staying with, and he recognized one of the names as a man he used to employ. He asked us to fetch him, and when we did he asked the man if he would be willing to hide him for a few days.

That particular man was really nice, and remembered that my cousin's husband had helped him in the past. Despite the fact that he could be killed for aiding a Tutsi, he took the risk and agreed to hide him. He took my cousin's husband to his house and hid him in the roof, but did not tell the rest of his family. He knew that if he told them they would tell other people and the Interhamwe would come.

My cousin's husband had a small radio with him, and was tracking the RPF location. Once he knew where the RPF was, he left at night to travel in their direction. He had told us that if we were still alive when the RPF came to stay nearby, he would come back for us. Even if there was shooting or fighting nearby, he told us to hide and wait so that he could find us.

When the RPF began getting close to the region we were in, the people we were working for decided to flee and forced us to go with them. There was a fear that the RPF would retaliate or attack anyone who was Hutu. They took us a long distance away. I was really worried. I kept telling the other girl that we needed to find a way to go back, because my cousin's husband would come looking for us and not be able to find us. The guy who had helped hide him remembered that my cousin's husband had promised to save him and his family because of his help. After a couple of days, he told me and the other girl that he would help us travel back.

We left during the night, without the others knowing, and returned to the place where we had been. The RPF had already come through the area and the Interhamwe had left, so it was now safe. It was just us and a couple of families who hadn't fled.

A few weeks passed with no sign of my cousin's husband. The family we had been working for eventually returned home, and we resumed working for them.

One day in July, on our way to fetch water, we saw my cousin's husband approaching with a group of RPF soldiers. I can remember feeling both relief and excitement. I couldn't believe the nightmare I had been living was actually over and that I no longer had to fear for my life. They took us with them, and the soldiers were very compassionate and caring. Butare was one of the last areas the RPF took over before the genocide fully ended and the country became safe.

The soldiers took us to a nearby school where we joined others who had survived, along with many who were injured and being cared for. They provided us with food and clothes. The three of us remained there together while my cousin's husband continued searching for information about the rest of his family. A few weeks later, he found out that his wife (my cousin) and all his kids were still alive but were scattered and staying in different places. He located a house for us to live in and brought us all there.

Once we moved to this new home and were living together, I began to think about going home. I believed without any doubt that my family must have survived as well and that I would be able to see them again soon. If we had all found ways to hide, I was certain that my family had done the same, or that they were safe because they had been in the church.

In Rwandan culture, adults did not typically explain what was happening to children or prepare them for things that were going to happen. Similarly, it was not considered proper for children to ask adults questions or make requests for things. So I continued to live with my cousin's family, waiting to see what would happen and if they would take me home.

One day my cousin told me that my brother was going to come. I had many siblings, so I asked which brother she was talking about. She told me it was my brother Emmanuel. I was very confused, as this was my oldest brother who had been living in Kenya before the genocide. They did not give me any details at the time, and all the confusion had a very negative impact on me. I still did not know where my family was, if they were dead or alive, why my brother was coming, or how he even knew where I was. At the time I hoped he was coming to pick me up and that we would then return to our house with my dad and the rest of my family.

I found out later that my cousin had gone on the radio and stated that I was still alive, and that if anyone from my family had survived, I was in Butare. After the genocide there were a lot of difficulties in reuniting family members and finding out who survived, so this was one of the methods used. My brother heard the radio broadcast and came to get me. He had first gone to Nyamata to look for my family and had been unable to find anyone. It had been taken over by the RPF in May, much earlier. He did not know anyone had survived until he heard that I was alive.

Emmanuel arrived at my cousin's house, and we all had dinner together. I was then sent to another room with my cousin's children while the adults talked. Before we went to bed my cousin told me that Ruth [her oldest child] and I needed to get our stuff ready, and that we were going to go with my brother to Kigali. Emmanuel wanted to take me with him, but he didn't want me to be by myself, so he arranged for Ruth, who was only two years younger than me, to come with us.

The next day we went to a small house in the city of Kigali that Emmanuel was renting with two friends who were soldiers. We stayed there, and he took us to start attending school. We didn't ask any questions, and he didn't tell us anything.

I started to figure out that my family had been killed. No one told me anything, but I remembered how, when Emmanuel came for me, my cousin was crying. Even when she sent us away to the room so the adults could talk, she was crying. When she came to tell us to get ready for Kigali she was still crying, and clearly devastated. I eventually decided not to even ask; that they must have been killed. I still believed that my second oldest brother was alive and must be somewhere in Rwanda. He was the one who had gone to Uganda before the genocide and was in the RPF. Again, I did not ask any questions about him. Emmanuel was so much older than me that we did not have a close relationship, and I suspect he had no idea I was going through these struggles.

The one thing I did find out was that Grace, who had saved me, was still alive. She and her four daughters made it safely to Burundi, and after the genocide they returned to Rwanda. They moved to a home close to my brother's place, and he took me to visit them. Grace was happy and relieved to see that I was alive and had survived the genocide.

In 1995, a year after the genocide, there was a commemoration in April, and we all went to Nyamata. I had still been told nothing, and no one had confirmed what had happened to my family. At the commemoration I saw my uncle, the one who had been with us when we were fleeing, and who I had sat near when we were gathered close to the church. He became very emotional when he saw me. I was not crying myself, but everyone else was. I finally truly understood that everyone in my family had been killed, along with thousands of others from the area.

The trauma of the genocide, what I had been through, and who I had lost was difficult to fully comprehend or really understand. It was so overwhelming that it was too much for me to think about, and I tried to block out the thoughts.

In 1996 I was sent away to attend a boarding school. The following year my brother went to Canada to go to university in Montreal. He received a visa to go and study but was unable to take me, so he planned for me to come over at a later point to join him. I continued to live at the boarding school, and on vacations would go and stay with my cousin in Butare. When my brother left for Canada, he never sat down and explained his choices or reasons for leaving. As a child you were just expected to trust that the decisions adults were making were what was best for you. I did not know where Canada was, or why my brother wanted us to go there. I was mad at the thought of leaving Rwanda.

When I was sixteen, four years after the genocide, I finally started to really understand what had happened to me. I was still living at the boarding school; I had friends who had also been through the genocide, and we would talk about it. When other kids had parents and siblings come visit them, I would feel depressed and alone. At night, I would go to bed and the trauma and images would come back. I started having severe nightmares and would scream in my sleep, see people, and hear the voices of those who had been killed.

In Rwanda there was no assistance available for those suffering from emotional and mental trauma. Counselling and therapy did not exist. When things became too extreme at school, when I was screaming and crying and couldn't sleep, they would take me to the hospital where I would receive shots to sedate me and allow me to sleep. I began to feel weird and different from the other students, and didn't want to talk about the genocide anymore. Most of the kids I was with, they had been through the genocide and had lost people, but not everyone; they still had siblings or parents alive. I was very alone—my only sibling still alive had not experienced the genocide and had moved to Canada. I felt a sense of shame and abandonment, and questioned why this had happened to me. When I would go to my cousin's home on school vacations, they would express and show me love, but I was unable to feel that love. I always felt like I didn't belong anywhere, and would ask God why her family had survived and my family had not. I acted out and was rebellious because I felt no one cared for me and did not know how to deal with the pain inside of me.

On one of my school vacations I went to visit my uncle, the one who had been at Nyamata. He had now remarried, but he had lost his wife and all eight of his kids in the genocide. I felt that he was the one person who could understand me; he was able to communicate with me in a way I could understand.

Over time I began to find out more about what had happened to my family and how they had been killed. The one thing I thanked God for was that I was not there to see those things. I have a cousin who had also been at Nyamata; he had been cut by machete and left to die. But he managed to survive the genocide, and told me what happened to my family and some of the things he had seen.

Another friend shared what had happened to my youngest brother, the baby of our large family. He was cut with machetes but did not die. He left the church and tried to find his way back to our house. He was only seven, and my friend saw him sitting there swollen and unable to walk. My friend would go and hide, and then would come back to check on my brother to see if he was still alive. The Interhamwe would come and cut my brother in more places with the machete—they wanted him to suffer and slowly bleed to death. Finally, my friend came back and found that my brother was completely dead.

After sharing this, Annick became very emotional and sat in silence for a long time. Eventually she was able to continue.

When I turned eighteen, I changed high schools so that I could be in Nyamata. I tried to cope with my trauma by becoming involved in survivor activities. I felt that my family was in the church. There were just bones of the victims there, but I thought I could somehow find a connection to my family that way. I would go to the church every day after school. I would touch the bones, and act as if they were people.

At my school I started an association of survivors of the genocide, and we would go do work at the church, cleaning and caring for it.

Around the region, work was also being done digging up the bodies that had been buried in mass pits. Survivors would come to identify their family members. Every time an excavation took place I would skip school, hoping they would find the bodies of my family. I can't fully express the disappointment I felt when I saw another survivor find the bodies of their family and I did not. For each body they unearthed, they would check the clothes and look in the pockets to try and find ID cards. I would go there day after day until a pit had been emptied. Then I would leave, depressed and upset. Many people thought I was going crazy.

I knew that my mom and one of my sisters had been killed in the church at Nyamata; my uncle was sure of this, even though we weren't able to identify their bodies. But no other family members were found. I prayed to God, asking for him to give me their bodies. When I would attend other funerals, I would feel jealous. They had found their family members and had been able to give them a proper burial. I felt that if I could find the body of at least one family member, then I could have a proper burial for them in the name of everyone who had been killed.

I went on like this for several years, and did not find them.

In 2002 I finished high school. My brother was trying to get a visa to allow me to come to Canada, but he wasn't having any success. My depression had continued to worsen; I was living day by day. The next year I received a visa to go to Belgium to attend post-secondary.

I stayed in Belgium for five years. I found that I could not focus at all on school. I was deeply wounded and depressed. I became known for my depression: "Annick who is depressed." I do not know why I found it so hard, or why it was so much more difficult for me than for some of my friends who had been through even worse experiences.

My brother came to visit me before I left for Belgium, and then again while I was living there. I did not return to Rwanda at all, and thought I never would.

In 2008 I finally received a visa to come to Canada, and joined my brother in Montreal. I was amazed at how everything in Canada was so big and huge! I couldn't believe the size of everything: the country, the houses, and the buildings. I had thought Belgium was paradise compared to Rwanda, but in Canada the scale of everything was amazing.

I had heard many good things about Canada before I came. The first thing I wanted to do was learn English. I couldn't speak a single word when I first arrived. I lived with my brother in Montreal for seven months before moving west. I made the decision to relocate to Calgary so that I would be fully immersed in English.

My first job was at Wendy's. I didn't understand anything in the interview, but still managed to get the job. It was a big adventure for me, but it helped me to learn the language very quickly. Someone would order a burger and ask for no pickles or mustard, and I wouldn't know what those words were in English, so I had to learn very fast.

Within six months I was able to move on to other jobs, and to understand enough English. I also experienced my first winter while living in Calgary. I did not have any boots so I decided to go to the mall; it was snowing but still sunny out, and I found this very confusing. By the time I reached the mall I couldn't even walk because my legs were so cold. I stood there in the mall crying because I was so shocked by the weather. During my first winter I think I called in sick every time it dropped to minus twenty.

After moving to Canada I continued to struggle with trauma and depression. During the months of April and May I would cut myself off from everyone and everything. I would go into a period of deep depression and isolation. Often I'd lose my job, or miss a month of classes. I wouldn't start to resume a normal life, or feel like myself again, until June.

In 2010 I returned to Rwanda for the first time to visit my uncle and attend some weddings. I also went to Nyamata and visited the church. In 2011 I moved back to Montreal to go to university. I again struggled with depression, and was on medication to help manage it and allow me to sleep. I struggled to focus in school, and didn't understand why I was having so many challenges that nobody else seemed to have. I didn't know anything about getting help or counselling. I hid what was going on from my brother and friends, and I lived alone because I didn't want anyone to see me in such a poor state.

In 2012 the urge to find my family and bury them returned. My brother Emmanuel had moved back to Rwanda; I phoned him, unable to suppress my anger, and accused him of not caring about their deaths.

We had never talked about the genocide or the loss of our family in detail. I didn't realize that he was traumatized as well, and that was why he couldn't discuss it. I felt the need to blame someone, and I directed it towards him.

I told him during the phone call that I needed to return to Rwanda in April and that I needed him to help me find our family. This is when he shared with me that he had already tried to find them. He explained that for those who were lucky, the Interhamwe would confess and say where the bodies were, but no one knew the location of our family members. He did not want me to come in April, as he did not think I would be able to handle it. But I had already bought a ticket.

I arrived on April 6. The next day I attended the official commemoration at Amahoro Stadium and witnessed how broken people were, as if the events had happened yesterday. I was numb, and didn't cry. During my visit I attended every commemoration event possible. After one of these events I returned to my brother's place, and as I was sitting in my room I started praying. I did not believe God existed. How could He allow this to happen to people, especially my father, who had served God for his entire life as a pastor? However, I was tired and emotionally exhausted, the radio was playing commemoration songs, and so I prayed to God, asking to know what my purpose was and to feel joy in my heart.

I asked some cousins on my mother's side, who were also survivors, for advice. They told me to focus on prayer, and suggested
some Bible verses. I started to attend church, but would cry through
the entire service. Then, one week before I was scheduled to return
to Canada, I was at church praying when I was overcome with feelings of peace and joy. I felt as if God were saying, "I loved you so
much that I kept you, among all the others who were killed." I felt I
was being told that I had a purpose in life: to bring hope to others.
I left Rwanda with a different point of view about the way I was living my life.

This was not the end of my struggles with mental health and
trauma. In 2013 I went through a severe depression and suffered
from suicidal thoughts. One night during the winter, I decided to
go outside. It was around nine p.m. I left my house with no jacket
on and aimlessly wandered the streets. A woman who knew me
was driving by and saw me; she took me to the hospital.

Despite these setbacks and struggles, the visit to Rwanda the previous year had changed me. I started to shift my perspective, and
believed the Bible verse that states everything works together for our
good. Even though I didn't know how things would work together
for my good, I started to believe that they eventually would.

I stopped asking, "Why wasn't I killed?" and began saying, "Why
did I survive?" I came to accept that the genocide had happened,
but that now I needed to look at what was next. I needed to move
forward. I realized that the best gift I could give myself would be forgiving those who had killed my family. I wanted to move on with my
life and catch up. I had lost so many years; I'd wasted them by being
held hostage by hatred.

Since the genocide ended I had carried around a feeling of
hatred for anyone who was Hutu, even babies and little children. I
felt that anyone who was a Hutu would grow up to become a killer.
When I saw Hutu children at school, I would say to them that if even
if they weren't killers, their parents had been. I placed the blame of

my family's death on anyone who was Hutu, even if they were not alive during the genocide or hadn't been involved. The feelings of hate were so large and encompassing that I grouped everyone into one category. Even here in Canada I was unable to even sit and talk with someone who was Hutu.

When I began to change I realized that I needed to let all of this go. I began the process of forgiving, and worked to escape this overwhelming hatred that had trapped me for so long.

By 2014 I finally found myself in a place where I was able to fully and completely forgive. During the process of forgiving, I began to steer my emotions in a new direction, towards loving those who are broken. I felt most strongly for survivors, as I knew the experience they had lived through, and that so many were still struggling with the trauma of the genocide. But I also found that it didn't matter where the person was from or what had happened. I felt connected to anyone who had experienced loss or trauma. I wanted to reach out to people who had lost hope.

When I returned to Rwanda that April, I spoke at a church for the first time. From there, I was invited by a woman to speak with another group of survivors about my journey to find forgiveness and healing. When I returned to Canada I began to speaking to groups here, starting with my local church. I realized that a story can be messy and ugly, but it can still help someone else. As I started speaking from my heart, I realized that this was my purpose now in life.

Now my goal is to help anyone who has experienced trauma or loss, or has felt hopeless. I want people to feel that they matter, because at one point in time I didn't feel as if my life mattered; I felt lost in the world. I want them to know that there is someone who supports them, who can offer a hug, and listen and talk.

I now feel Rwandan first and Canadian second. Living in Canada has helped me learn who I am and what I am capable of. I've gained a lot of confidence and found my footing. I have learned about the rights and freedoms an individual should have, and that people don't have the right to do whatever they want to others.

I have taken on many Canadian traits, and I notice this the most when I visit Rwanda. I treat people differently and have different expectations. I now find things like bartering over prices very awkward because I am no longer used to it, and I've forgotten small nuances of Rwandan culture. I also miss the hot showers and comforts I am now used to in Canada, which are not always available in Rwanda.

One day I would like to move back to Rwanda—because of the beautiful weather and the food, and because my goal is to help people who have lost hope and feel alone. You can support someone financially, but they will still struggle inside without emotional support. Many people are still struggling with forgiveness and moving on with their lives, and they need this emotional support.

Six

Beatrice

The longest distance I travelled for an interview was to the little town of Watson Lake, Yukon, about three hours east of White-horse. There I met Beatrice, who welcomed me with incredible hos-pitality, insisting that I cancel my hotel and stay with her. She'd show me around the town, she said, and introduce me to some of her friends. Beatrice's geniality, her mannerisms, her way of addressing those we met, her connectedness to community—it was all distinctly Rwandan. As we walked through the town people would continually come over to say hello; I had the feeling that she knew everyone there. This carried on the next day when I gave Beatrice a ride to White-horse. Every time we stopped somewhere people would smile and greet her by name.

One thing many people notice when they travel to Rwanda is how friendly everyone is—a striking contrast to our North American individualism. Given our attachment to technology, the greater amount of time we spend indoors, and our tendency to avoid eye contact let alone conversations with strangers, there's a greater sense of distance and sterility. But in Rwanda, whether you're in a rural community or the capital city, you rarely pass people without an acknowledgment or a greeting. Any outing involves stopping to talk with at least one person. Even conversations with complete strangers include handshakes and jokes, a sense of openness and familiarity.

Beatrice has an indomitable spirit. In the short time I was with her I could feel the strength of character she radiated. And as she told me stories of her experiences elsewhere in Canada, it became clear that wherever she'd lived she'd found a way to connect, to form a sense of community. After I met one of her friends, a young Filipino woman married to a much older man, Beatrice told me about some of the girl's struggles; she worried about her feeling isolated. It was clear that she'd taken this young woman under her wing and was working to help her however she could.

Beatrice's empathy and huge heart were evident. She'd never be rich as long as there were people in poverty needing assistance, she told me; at the time, she was in the process of filling a shipping container with clothes and other items to send to a refugee camp in Rwanda. She wouldn't allow her remote location, her life circumstances (she'd recently been laid off), or her own personal challenges to become barriers against helping others. With such a complex life, and with such a quirky sense of humour, Beatrice remains one of the most compelling people I've ever had the chance to meet.

Beatrice's Story

My mom was very sick after my birth, so I was given to my grandma to be cared for. We had a large extended family, and Grandma had raised more kids than it was possible to count. Her family had been scattered and torn apart during the chaos of 1959, which resulted in many family members and grandkids ending up in her care. I was very spoiled as a child because I lived with many old people who took care of me. I was a baby, the only kid, and everybody else was grown up and much older, except my cousins, who would occasionally visit on holidays.

My first memories are from when I was five or six years old. It was 1973 and there was a war going on. Everyone was fired from their jobs, and people were dying from the attacks and violence. Many family members came to stay with my grandma (who I called Mama), and some were killed. They sent me to live with a different family in order to hide me and keep me safe. One of my older cousins had a job working with a white family, and was the only person who still had employment. She was forced to take on the role of financially supporting everyone in the family. It was extremely tough on her, and a difficult and scary time for everyone.

Despite the chaos of my early childhood, I remained unaware of the ethnic division that existed in our country. It wasn't until I attended school that I noticed anything. In class they would ask us to stand up according to our ethnicity, and somehow I knew to stand up when they called for Tutsi. However, many other students did not know their ethnicity. There was a girl who was Hutu but had many friends who were Tutsi, and she would stand up at the same time as us. Outside of school, these terms remained meaningless. All of us played together regardless of ethnicity.

I was young, and found everything about life amazing and interesting. There was a white family who would send me nice things like shoes and candy. Life overall was enjoyable, and I had a good childhood.

I was a really bright child, and my grandma decided to keep me occupied and busy by sending me to a literacy program that was being run by the Seventh-Day Adventist church. It was technically for older adults who didn't know how to read and write, but it was located close to our home. The priest who taught the class was really impressed by me. He contacted the local elementary school and made arrangements for me to attend. They put me immediately into grade three, skipping the two lower grades. This led to some problems for me when I first started school, as the only way I knew how to write was using capital letters. That is what they had taught us at the literacy program, and by skipping two grades I missed this instruction at school. I initially feared going to school because I received beatings from the teacher, who expected everyone to write using lowercase letters with proper spelling.

Eventually I found my place and loved school. I got on well with the teachers, and was known for my ability with numbers.

Most of the teachers at school were Hutu, but my teacher in my final year of primary school was one of the few Tutsi teachers and also the school principal. He was the whole reason our village had been given a school, and was the type of teacher who loved and cared for his students. I will never forget him. In class I would often solve questions in a different way. Rather than questioning or criticizing my methods, he would come and sit with me and learn the way I had solved the question. It's terrible to know that he and many of his children were killed during the genocide by a community he had done so much for.

At the end of primary school I wanted to continue on to high school, but in order to do this we had to take an exam. The exam pissed me off because only a certain number of those who wanted to go to high school were permitted to go. In my class, only two Tutsi students passed and were accepted into the government school. It was very frustrating, as I desperately wanted to continue my schooling.

We found out that the Presbyterian church was going to be opening a private high school and that they were looking to recruit forty-five students. Despite being Catholic, I was sent along with quite a few other students from my region. I passed the examination and was accepted. It was a very long distance from my home and in a different province, so I travelled there alone, as it was too difficult for anyone to accompany me. When I arrived I discovered that it was not a boarding school like we had assumed, and there were no accommodations. The director of the school was a Presbyterian priest, and when he realized that six of us had arrived with nowhere to stay, he asked us all to live in his house. He was an exceptional man who really cared about the school and the students. They had accepted sixty students thinking that some would drop out and bring the numbers to forty-five. When this didn't happen, he decided to let all sixty students attend so that no one would be turned away. He was such a good man, and didn't have the heart to send anyone away.

In the second semester they fired him. They accused him of being corrupt because he sometimes drank. After the genocide questions about him kept haunting me. I felt that I needed to find him and, in some way, thank him for everything he had done for me. It took several years to find him, and when I did I went with a friend to visit him and his family. I was so lucky that I did, as shortly thereafter he passed away. But I felt good because I was able to connect with him again, take gifts for his family, and express my gratitude.

Throughout the rest of high school I found places to live with other classmates, and eventually rented a home with other students. I finished high school fourth in my class, but I was unable to get a scholarship for university. I had converted to Presbyterianism in order to continue at the school, and after graduating I kept attending the church. I liked to give the priest a hard time, as I knew he felt guilty that I hadn't been able to go on to university. Anytime he saw me at the end of the service he would ask if I had found a job yet, and I would always say no. He would tell me that we needed to pray, and I went along with it. I kept telling him that I had no job even though I did, just to tease him. I enjoyed it [laughter].

In 1988 I got a job working for a businessman who was the main supplier for the Ministry of Education. I worked there for some time, but I wasn't a good fit for the position and eventually resigned and moved on. I was able to get another job as the first accountant at the tourism office, a government department attached to the office of the president.

When I first started working there it was extremely difficult because I was Tutsi. The other employees would talk about me and call me names, and question what a Tutsi was doing coming to work there. I stood up to them, and after a few months things started to improve. I was very open and socialized with everyone because I talk a lot, and gradually they accepted me. A lot of the other employees were young like me, and we would have gatherings on the weekends where we would get together to eat and drink. I hosted many of these at my house, and one weekend I suggested we organize a trip to Burundi. I enjoyed travelling, and would often go to the Congo to do my shopping. I told the others that we were young and that this was the time to have such adventures. The next long weekend a group of us gathered together and travelled to Burundi.

While we were away the police intelligence of the province began making accusations that we had gone to Burundi because we were members of the RPF. I had no clue that this was happening, or that they would make these accusations. It never came to mind to figure out who was among our group or what ethnicity they were. The security intelligence officer wrote a note to the president claiming that I was an accomplice and was collaborating with the *inyenzi*, the name given to Tutsi opponents of the government, and that this is why I had brought everyone to Burundi. When I came back from the trip I received an urgent phone call from a friend who worked in the capital.

"We are writing a letter to fire you."

"For what?" I asked.

"You took people to Burundi and they're joining a negative movement," he responded. He used the word "cockroaches" to describe them. I knew that this could not be good.

When I'm afraid, I run, don't ask me why. But whenever I am afraid and don't feel peace within me, even if we are just having a conversation like this, I take off. At the time of the phone call I was in the office at work. I put down everything, went home, dressed, and took a car immediately to my family's house in Kigali because I was afraid.

My dad worked for the army as a mechanic, and had already learned the news. He had started looking for higher-ranking officers who could intervene. As soon as I arrived home I went to see him.

"I'm trying to fight this," he told me.

I interrupted him. "Daddy, don't even try. I never did it. If you keep asking people what is going on, they will think it is true and that every family member is involved. Leave them. They're making up a story, and if they have to kill someone, they will kill me alone. But if you continue to ask questions, then all of us will be targets. So please leave it!"

I stayed in Kigali with my family and never returned to my job. I abandoned the house I had been renting, leaving behind all my possessions. The police continued to track and follow my movements, but they had no evidence—and I really didn't care. I knew that if they wanted to kill me they would kill me, and there was nothing I could do to prevent it. I was innocent and had done nothing wrong. I never talked again to those I had travelled with, so I don't know what happened to them or if they faced similar situations.

I began searching for a new job and heard that a mining agency was hiring. I went for an interview with the director. When he asked why I had left my previous job, I just told him that there had been things I had disagreed with. He laughed at my response and said, "If you don't agree with me, I will fire you too," then asked if I knew how to type. I completed a typing test, and then left to go home.

I assumed I hadn't gotten the job, so never went back to check. One day someone saw me in the street and told me the director had been looking for me, so I returned to the office. I met with his assistant and told her the story. Apparently I could have been hired for her position, but when the director couldn't find me he hired her instead. However, the director of production (a different department) was also looking to hire an assistant and agreed to take me on. It was my third job, and the last job I worked before the genocide.

Maybe everything happens for a reason—the events at work in a way helped save my life. I had been threatened, called a cockroach, and accused of things at my previous job. At my new job I was treated poorly by my boss. He didn't like me, and intentionally interfered and lied to prevent me from getting raises. These experiences made me fearful and unsettled. So when the RPF attacked Rwanda on October 1st, 1990, my immediate thought was that I would be a target and needed to flee the country. I left for Burundi three days later, and it ended up saving me.

OCTOBER 1, 1990

On the first day of the attack a roadblock was set up right outside my home. I was scared to death. My mind went straight back to 1973, when I was a young child and killings had taken place. I felt that I was the walking dead.

From the time they attacked until the day I left, I never slept. I went to work and felt as if everybody was staring at me and thinking things. I was in a permanent state of fear; everything scared me. I told a Tutsi coworker that I needed to leave the country. I said, "Whether they win or lose—I see death. I don't see anything else. I must leave." I asked her to tell everyone I was sick if I failed to show up for work, so that they wouldn't suspect I was fleeing.

The night before I left I gathered with some friends at a local hotel for a grilled brochette and told them that I was planning on leaving the country to go to Burundi. But before I could finish explaining myself, an announcement on the radio interrupted me. They were listing a new set of rules for the country, prohibiting gatherings and imposing a curfew. When the announcer finished listing the new restrictions, I turned to my friends and said, "We are dead." I was afraid I was going to be killed before I even had a chance to flee the country. We all left the hotel in a rush without paying. We didn't want to draw any attention to ourselves or call the waiter, as it was now illegal for us to be there as a group. All the taxis and buses had stopped running, so we each had a long walk to get home from the hotel.

When I finally got home, I took only the lightest clothes I had, and a handbag. I didn't want anybody to suspect I was leaving, so I didn't pack a suitcase. I was living with two of my brothers and a younger sister. I asked a friend to take my sister to stay with my mom, and gave both my brothers money and told them to try and get travel documents to join me in Burundi. There were two buses that regularly travelled between Kigali and Bujumbura in Burundi, and I made it just in time to catch the last bus. I was very lucky, as after I left they shut these buses down.

Late that night the bus arrived at the border of Rwanda and Burundi. We were required to disembark and individually go through border control. As I lined up to wait for my turn I was so scared that I was shaking. I watched a Rwandan who had driven a car go through the process. He had parked his car and was at border control. The agent stamped his passport but directed him to another office to have his car cleared. At some point one of the officials must have stated that the man was on the blacklist, and he overheard. He immediately abandoned his car and started running for the border. The guards on the Burundi side ran out to help rescue him. I watched as this happened and kept thinking to myself, "This is my end." I was certain I was not going to make it across.

When it was my turn to talk to the border agent I told him that I was going to Bujumbura to care for a sick cousin. He wanted to know where my cousin lived, so I made up an address and gave it to him. I didn't have a paper approving my absence from work, and he accused me of lying about having permission to travel. I insisted that I had forgotten the paper at home. Eventually he stamped my passport and let me go.

By the time I reached Bujumbura I had not slept in days and was talking nonsense from the exhaustion and the stress. Everyone in Burundi wanted news about Rwanda, but I didn't know what to tell them. I usually talk too much, but I had no words now. The world became dark. I was admitted to the hospital, where I spent several weeks.

When I was released from the hospital I drifted between places. I stayed for some time with other people I had met on the bus, and also with a cousin. I was twenty-four years old, with no job, no contact with my family, and only the few items I had brought with me.

Eventually I decided to try and go to university. A friend had given me money to exchange for her, but because I had fled Rwanda I hadn't been able to return the money and had no way to send it back. I used this to pay for school and made it through my first year. After that I ran out of money, so I had to quit and look for work.

A man in a prayer meeting I attended directed me to the Anglican church; they were looking for an assistant. I had to take a test that required I type on a computer. It was my first time seeing a computer, but I knew how to type, so I passed the test and was given the position. After that my life improved. I was able to rent a house, buy some things, and start to return to being myself. My landlady lived in a rural area, so every month when she came to pick up the rent she would bring me beans, potatoes, and bananas. We soon became friends. I also started to attend the Anglican church and met another friend, who was a teacher and also taught Sunday school. Life started to be life again. I had a good job, and friends who I could count on.

My two brothers I had been living with in Kigali eventually came over and joined me. Things were very dangerous in Rwanda now: Tutsi were being attacked and killed on a daily basis. I was following what was happening on the radio and was very worried about my mom, and that she would die of hunger.

When the Arusha Peace Agreement was signed in 1993 [between the RPF and the Rwandan government], I decided it would be safe to send my youngest brother back to Rwanda to take money to our mom. I stitched the money to the inside of his pants and sent him to go see her. A lot of people disapproved of this decision. I kept silent and ignored everyone's criticism, but I was worried. I had not been taking the time to pray or focus on God, but now I started praying to myself: "God, what will happen? I need to find my younger brother. And I need to find that woman who I took money from. I'm not asking for other relatives; I know that everybody will die in Rwanda, but please perform a miracle. If those two people die before I see them again, I will die badly."

My brother stayed in Rwanda after returning, but what I prayed for eventually happened. I had prayed that he would survive even if he had to die later. He had to at least survive until I saw him again, and in the end he did.

Life in Burundi was very difficult, as there was a civil war going on as well, and both Tutsi and Hutu were being killed. I looked for ways to try and leave the country but there was no way to escape, as I didn't have a passport and wasn't recognized as a refugee.

The president of Burundi was killed in the same crash as the president of Rwanda, and it only worsened the situation. Sometimes I had to go into hiding to stay safe, but only temporarily. The area I lived in was only for Tutsi, so it was fairly secure. People lived in a very segregated way, in areas either for Hutu or for Tutsi. Sometimes there would be road closures and violence, but it wasn't as bad as what was occurring in Rwanda.

I continued to work in the Anglican church, and also ran a small shop selling anything I could find. When the Anglican missionaries would go to visit the rural areas, I would always ask them to bring me back certain items that were difficult to find in Bujumbura, and I'd sell or trade them.

As the genocide went on, the RPF began liberating and securing areas of Rwanda, piece by piece. At the time I had eight people staying with me in a two-room house. It was a very difficult situation, as the civil war was still going on in Burundi and there was nowhere else for them to stay. In June the RPF began encouraging people to return to the areas of the country that had been liberated, so I decided to rent a vehicle and take everyone back to Rwanda.

I took those who had been staying with me and dropped them off in Rwanda. We saw lots of dead bodies and destruction on the way. After that I travelled to a refugee camp that had been set up in the town of Kabuga. I helped transport some people I knew at the camp back to their homes. When I reached the edge of Kigali, someone let me know that my brother had survived and directed me to the refugee camp he was in. The RPF had liberated Kigali while I was in the country. After that I returned alone to Burundi; I needed to finish up my work and hand everything over. I fully moved back to Rwanda in September 1994.

It is difficult to count how many family members were killed in the genocide. My dad had four wives, including my mom, and more than twenty kids. Of the kids, only three survived. My dad was also killed. My mom survived, but she was in such bad condition that she died shortly after the genocide. The same thing occurred with many family members on my mom's side: they survived the genocide but were so badly injured or ill that they died after it ended.

In the years following the genocide, occasional attacks on Tutsi still occurred. My younger brother, who I had prayed to survive, was killed by a grenade attack one year after I returned to Rwanda. I refused to cry when it happened, because what I had prayed for had come true. He had survived the genocide and I had been able to see him again.

When I got back to Rwanda I was able to use my experience in Burundi to negotiate a job with the Anglican church. They were unable to pay me but provided food and housing. I worked for them for three years, and then they paid for me to attend college in Kenya. I decided to study journalism, and when I completed my studies I returned to Rwanda. I resumed my work with the church for another two years and then took a job working for a German non-profit. When that position ended I started up my own newspaper called *Heritage in Rwanda*. I was advocating for the poor, helping others, and caring for my family members who were still alive. The stress was very difficult to handle and I became very ill, worse than when I had fled Rwanda and arrived in Burundi.

I started looking for other countries to move to and discovered two of the most beautiful countries in the world: Switzerland and Canada. I decided on Canada because even before I decided to leave Rwanda I had wanted to visit there. When my newspaper was not generating enough income, I would take side jobs working for different international agencies, and my boss at one of these was from Quebec; he had shared wonderful stories about Canada. I also wanted to move to a place where I could learn and improve my English.

I came to Canada in 2004, arriving in St. Catharines, Ontario. I went to school and studied accounting and hospitality management. It was winter when I arrived, and sometimes I would go without eating just so that I could take a taxi or a bus to school and avoid walking outside. One of the things I found most surprising when I first arrived was seeing the sun out even when it was cold—I had always thought that if the sun was out it would be warm. I kept telling the people back home about this.

One of the hardest parts of moving to Canada was learning to live alone. Before coming here, I had never lived alone. I also didn't know how to cook and wasn't used to doing cleaning. It was a change for me to be alone and cook for myself.

I eventually moved to Fort Erie to attend Niagara College, finishing in 2008. Next I continued my studies at Niagara University in Buffalo, commuting across the border; I graduated in 2010. After I finished, I spent six months travelling and getting to know Canada.

I was offered a job while I was visiting the Northwest Territories but turned it down. I started regretting that decision, and did some research. That is when I discovered the Yukon and decided it was a good location to look for work, with accessible roads for travel. At the time my friends in Ontario thought I was crazy, but now I have lived here for five years. I like nature and the simple life, and I've fallen in love with the Territories.

I love Canada, but even if I forced myself, I can't be more Canadian than Rwandan. Most of my money goes towards plane tickets and frequent visits back to Rwanda. The one thing that I feel is lacking here is the strong sense of community. In Rwanda we "belong" in a way that doesn't exist here.

Living here has changed my opinion on many things. Before I came, I had this perception that white people loved money before everything else. But now that view has changed. I also have great respect for the government. Even if a poor leader is elected there are protections in place that prevent this from damaging or destroying the country. You have very smart people and a well-run country.

The structure of Canada's government is something we should export to Rwanda.

What I love most about Canada is how positive the nation is. Canada was the first multicultural country I'd been to. I really appreciate and love this aspect of Canada. In Rwanda, it used to be Tutsi or Hutu. Today it is a bit different, and you will see people from all over the world in Rwanda.

I still struggle with English, but I read constantly. For me, everything is connected to a sense of morality. When I read something that touches morality I will always succeed at understanding it. If there is no morality in something I will fail to understand it; the English disappears for me. I know that as long as there are those who are in need, I will never be wealthy. That is my path in life.

Seven

Clement

In Rwanda today, the government is promoting the idea that everyone is Rwandese. Although most Rwandans still know how they'd
be classified, it isn't something that's openly discussed. When I meet
Rwandans, I generally have no idea what their official "ethnicity"
is. Of all the Tutsi I've met, only a handful conform to the original
colonial description.

Clement is one of these. He's tall and lanky; his build and other
features easily fit the stereotype. Throughout the genocide, physical
characteristics were used to incite and encourage attacks, with radio
stations like the RTLM calling upon killers to cut down the "tall trees."

Despite his harrowing past, Clement is a jokester, a continuing
source of smiles and laughs. He frequently tells me that if I continue
to eat goat I will grow a beard, and he's somehow convinced that
I'll learn Kinyarwanda despite my inability to remember even basic
greetings.

Clement doesn't understand the Canadian obsession with cold
foods; once, he'd even tried to microwave ice cream just to warm
it up. He'd also mentioned that pizza was one of his favourites, so
I ordered one and stopped to pick it up on my way to meet him.
But when I arrived he suggested that we wait to eat until after the
interview. It was telling. The pizza would get cold, but for Clement it
was more important to share his experiences first. Only then could
we comfortably socialize.

Clement's Story

I was raised in a family of twelve, with nine brothers and sisters. I was the seventh child, with two younger sisters. There was a big range in our ages, and many of my siblings were always away from home attending schools. At the time most high schools were boarding schools, so students would only be home on school holidays to see their families.

My happiest memories as a child are from the holidays we spent together. With such a big family, events like Christmas and Easter were full of warmth and wonderful moments. I was a happy and innocent kid who feared nothing, not even butchering a goat or a chicken for meals. On important holidays we would often get to slaughter a goat to make brochettes, and I always wanted to be the one to kill it. Butchering our own meat and preparing our food was just a normal part of my childhood.

When my dad was not home I had the responsibility of watching the cows on the farm and taking care of them. I loved this task, but my dad was always worried that I would lose interest in school because of how much I loved working with the cows. He had been barred from attending medical school due to his ethnicity, and he didn't want us to end up like him; he wanted us to go as far as we could in our education.

I realized I was Tutsi for the first time at school when I was around the age of eight. The teacher asked us to stand up based upon our ethnic roots. At the time, I knew that there were Tutsi and Hutu but I didn't know what I was. I stood up for Hutu, like most of the other students, but one of my classmates said it was a lie and that I was Tutsi. When I returned home from school that day I asked my parents about this, but they refused to give me a straight answer. Eventually I ended up asking my uncle, and he was the one who confirmed that I was Tutsi. Despite the discrimination against us, he instilled a confidence in me that being Tutsi was something good, that it was not something I should be ashamed of.

I was friends with students from both ethnicities, as none of us really understood the purpose of the labels. However, after the teacher started classifying us into groups, we started to look at each other differently. As I progressed through school I began to face a lot of bullying from my classmates. They bullied those of us who were Tutsi, because we were the minority and considered different from them. I did not enjoy confrontations and was a good student, but found myself forced to fight to defend myself. The teachers and principals didn't view bullying as a problem, so the only way to protect my dignity and make other students respect me was to fight back against them. In many ways, that is how I think the genocidal ideology started: in the classroom, by dividing children.

APRIL 6, 1994

I was at home the night the president's plane was shot down. At the time, there were seven of us children there, along with my parents. One of my brothers left that night with a visitor, his classmate, and he never came back. He was killed at some point after this. When the genocide ended we spent a long time searching for his body; we talked with prisoners who had been killers and searched for someone who had witnessed his death. We finally found his remains in 2009 and gave him a proper burial.

My uncle came to our home the following morning, on April 7th, and told us that the president was dead, and that his plane had been shot down. He told us he had dreamt that there would be a war, and that we were all going to die. Prior to this we had known something bad was building and that Interhamwe were being trained, but we also knew there was nothing we could do about it, so we had just carried on with our lives.

Some of my family members were optimistic: they thought there might be a change and things may improve now that the president was dead. Many people had started to hate him, and were not his fans anymore. They had lived through a similar experience when the president had taken power through a coup d'état in 1973.

Tutsi had been displaced and threatened, but it was only for a short time. Many people were expecting the same thing to occur—that the tension and threats would stop in a few days. I was only eleven at the time and really didn't understand what was going on or why it was happening.

We stopped sleeping in the house after the president was killed. Every night we would walk outside to the forest around the house or to the banana plantation to sleep. We would try to hide ourselves because it was often during the night when there was the greatest risk of people coming to kill us.

From that time onwards, things deteriorated. It became clear that there was a lot of tension between us and our neighbours in the region. People were saying that Tutsi were the enemy of the country, and neighbours started to look at us that way. Information was being spread over the radio claiming that the Tutsi had a plan to kill all the Hutu. Most people were illiterate at the time, especially in rural areas, and the radio was the primary source of information and news. During the broadcasts they would terrify people by claiming that Tutsi had prepared barrels of oil to fry Hutu babies, that we had already dug pits to bury the bodies, or planned to dump the bodies into latrines. The divisive message being spread to Hutu everywhere in the country was that "We have to kill them before they kill us." People accepted this information as fact, and individuals who may have considered themselves good Christians became merciless beasts, attacking their neighbours.

On April 19th our house was burned down. One or two nights before, a group of local leaders had shown up and searched the house, accusing us of possessing guns and radios to communicate with rebel soldiers. Our friends, our good neighbours whom we shared everything with, were accusing us of betraying them and being their enemies.

When they returned to burn the house—it was around nine in the morning—we were inside and saw the attackers coming. We were forced to run, along with my uncle's family, who lived next door, and all our nearby Tutsi neighbours. Somehow we managed to stay together, and went up on a mountain where we could see what was happening. The attackers were a group of people from our region. They spent most of the day looting and burning the homes in the area. They didn't bother to come for us, as they knew we would be killed later in the day.

In the afternoon we could still see the flames and smoke from our house. I became very worried about what had happened to my pet cow I had left in the house. I snuck back to our home to check on her. Everything was so burned and damaged that I couldn't recognize anything. Then I saw our cow, our friendly pet, unable to walk. Her back legs had been cut at the knees to prevent us from being able to take her. She was alive but in an immense amount of pain. I wasn't able to process what I was seeing. It was a traumatizing and horrifying moment. But what I didn't know was that the worst was yet to come.

That evening they came to attack us on the mountain where we had gathered. The local Hutu were being led by an Interhamwe soldier, and they were singing and shouting that they "knew our plan." My uncle had a Bible and was praying, so we all closed our eyes and started to pray. I was too terrified to keep my eyes closed; I opened them and saw the killers coming towards us. I grabbed the hands of my two younger sisters, who were seven and nine, and started running. I don't know which way I ran or what direction I went—I was in a panic, just running for my life. The others were still praying and didn't know what was happening. That was the last time I saw most of them.

One of my deepest regrets, and something I will always feel guilty about, is that I didn't try and alert more people. One of the other boys was the same age as me. We had been classmates and went through the bullying at school together. I considered him a brother and blame myself for his death. His entire family died in the genocide. If I had just grabbed him and pulled him away with me, I am convinced that he would have survived. It is something that still haunts and traumatizes me today.

It was raining out and beginning to get dark, so I pulled my sisters towards a nearby house to shelter us from the rain. I didn't know who lived there, and after a few minutes I was consumed by intense fear and decided we should move. We briefly sought shelter in a banana plantation, but again I became scared, and we began walking again, unsure of where to go. At some point a family friend, who was Hutu, saw us passing by and called out to get our attention. She took us to her home, and we stayed there for the night. Some of her family lived next door, and the next morning they demanded that she send us away. She was very scared, and also wanted to avoid confrontation with them. If the Interhamwe were to find out she was harbouring us, they would kill her. I regret never having had the chance to properly thank her for what she did for us that night. She passed away before I could visit.

That morning as we were preparing to leave, I thought I saw my mom in the distance. I left my sisters with the woman and went to check if it was her. Somehow my mom had survived the attack the previous evening and had managed to escape. In the time it took for me to reach her it became too dangerous to go back and get my sisters. My mom insisted that we leave and said that my sisters would be able to find us later.

We decided to travel to a church called Kabgayi that was in the centre of the country. It was a very big church, so we felt it would be a good place to hide and that we would be safe there. The church was seventy to eighty kilometres away, so we began the long journey to walk there. At some point my grandmother joined us. I am not sure how she found us, but I assume it was because there was only one way to travel to the church, and people had told her where we were.

Halfway to the church we found ourselves unable to continue. Until that point we had travelled by road, going from the home of one friend to the next in order to stay safe on the journey. We had passed by the home of a distant relative, and they had warned us that the Interhamwe had set up roadblocks everywhere, making it impossible to travel any farther.

We ended up going to stay in the home of a Tutsi family my mom was friends with. My two younger sisters who we had left behind and my fifteen-year-old sister arrived and joined us there. The neighbourhood they lived in was primarily Tutsi, so attacks and killings hadn't started yet. The Hutu in the region did not yet know what they "had to do," that they were supposed "to kill all Tutsi." However, word spread quickly. By the end of our fourth day, killings started and we became targets once again.

The house was in a good location because it was on top of a mountain and all the surrounding homes were occupied by Tutsi. Close to two hundred people had gathered in the area, and everyone worked together to try to resist attacks by the local Hutu. Initially the attackers were not very organized, so the attacks were unsuccessful. There were very few deaths. We fought them off using stones or any other materials we could find.

Eventually the killers became organized and were strengthened by the arrival of the Interhamwe. They spread a false message, claiming that an airplane was going to fly over and check if the Tutsi had been killed; anyone who was Tutsi should burn something like a cattle house so that the smoke would make it look like everyone had already been killed. Many Tutsi believed the rumour and followed the instructions, which allowed the killers to identify where the Tutsi were located so that they could be killed.

We knew we would have to leave or we would be killed. My mom wanted me to travel to the home of another family friend, but I refused to go alone. Instead, my older sister stayed with me and we fled in one direction while my grandmother, mom, and younger sisters went off in other directions. All four survived the genocide, but I do not know how, as we were separated from that point onwards. We were very fortunate to leave when we did—the next day the mountain was attacked again, and it was very successful. All the people in the surrounding area were killed, as well as the people from the home where we had been staying.

When my sister and I fled the mountain we were running, not

really knowing what direction we were headed. We were extremely thirsty, so we looked for a house to go and ask for water. When we entered the house the national radio was playing a speech by Dr. Théodore Sindikubwabo, who had been appointed as the interim president. In the speech he talked about how we were in an emergency situation and it was not a time to joke—that you should not joke with Tutsi; it was time to work. In Rwanda, the term "work" was a euphemism for killing Tutsi that had been around since 1959. His speech was being broadcast and spread everywhere, worsening the situation for Tutsi. I can remember this moment so clearly. The man who was the president of the country that I was a citizen of was telling the nation to kill me.

Two days later, on a Saturday, my sister and I were still walking, and we had a Bible and songbook in our hands. Along the way we passed by a church where people were gathered, singing. We knew the song being sung and thought that maybe the people at the church would be willing to help us. A woman coming out of the church spotted us with our songbook and Bible and invited us to come in and join them. At the end of the church service she took us with her to her home. She said it was clear we were travelling alone, and asked where we were coming from and where we were headed. We trusted her, and told her the truth. She gave us food and water, and we prayed together. She asked two men from the church to go with us to our destination, about twenty kilometres away, to make sure we made it safely.

Without their help it is unlikely we would have made it. The road was full of blood. We could see people being killed and others begging for mercy. It was a densely populated area; the only way to travel was by road. The killers constantly asked the two men accompanying us if we were Tutsi, and they always said no. We were fortunate to be too young to have identity cards—there was no proof that we were Tutsi, and the killers believed the men. If we had been adults we would have been killed.

We arrived, with the help of the men, at the house of some Hutu friends. It was very dangerous, so we had to stay in the house and avoid being seen. The area was full of Hutu refugees, over four thousand, who were fleeing the war between the government soldiers and the RPF. Many of them were extremists—they would kill anyone they thought was Tutsi, even local Hutu who they felt looked too much like a Tutsi.

We stayed in this location for over two months. Two of my brothers joined us. One of them was twenty-four years old, and he took over the role of guiding us and making decisions. Without him, things would have been very different.

By the end of June, the RPF was approaching the region. Everyone decided to leave—they feared the RPF and thought they would be killed for being Hutu if they stayed. But the direction they would be travelling would have required us to pass back through the region we were from. This would have been really risky, as Hutu people would have recognized us; we would become targets and be killed. So we decided to go in the opposite direction, in the direction of the RPF.

As we travelled, we arrived in a village that was completely deserted: there were no people, and no soldiers from either side. Everyone in the area had fled. We spotted a woman in a house across the street and went to ask for water. From the way she was talking it became clear that she was mentally ill, which was probably why she was the only one still in the village. She wasn't dangerous to us and we weren't a danger to her, so we asked if we could stay, and she agreed.

We stayed with her for about a week, until her family and many others returned to the village. There was a Tutsi woman who was living with one of the returning men. She was being held against her will, a common occurrence during the genocide. Tutsi women were often taken hostage; some men would abuse and rape them, and then kill them. Others were taken as sex slaves and held hostage for the duration of the genocide. That was how they survived. The Tutsi woman warned us that the family of the woman we were staying with had made plans to kill us the next night.

We left that evening, and again headed in the direction where we thought the RPF soldiers might be. It was a strange time. We didn't know what things were like in the rest of the country, or for our family members. We didn't know if we were the only survivors, if everyone had died, or what. On the journey we met with another family who were also attempting to reach the RPF. Eventually we numbered around twenty people. There was no clear idea which direction we should travel in, so we just followed our instincts and hoped for the best.

After several hours of travelling we reached the location of the RPF. It was a surprise for them, as seeing Tutsi survivors was not a frequent occurrence. They asked us why we had come there, and we explained that we were worried we were going to die so had come to them for protection. The soldiers started to find other survivors coming from different directions, and eventually brought us all together and made a camp. My brother asked the soldiers if they could escort him to rescue the Tutsi woman who had helped us. The next morning they went and were able to bring her back to the refugee camp.

We stayed at the camp with other refugees for several weeks. During this time, peace progressively came to the rest of the country as the RPF gained control.

Sometime in August we left the camp and travelled to the location of another family friend who lived around forty kilometres from where our family home had been. Since our house had been burned down, there was no place for us to go. Everything was destroyed. That same month our mom and younger sisters came and joined us there.

We lived with this friend for a long time, until April of 1995. Over this time, we gradually started hearing about other people we knew who had survived.

One year after we fled our family home, we journeyed back to it. What is strange is that it was on the exact same day we had left—April 19th. I remember this because I wrote the day down so that I wouldn't forget. All that was left of our home was one door.

We gradually rebuilt it and moved back. Out of our family of twelve, eight of us survived the genocide. My three older brothers lived elsewhere, but myself and my two younger sisters lived with our parents in the rebuilt home. After the genocide my goal was to return to school. I even naively asked the neighbours if they had taken or knew the whereabouts of my schoolbooks.

When I finished primary school and began high school, things changed. As a teenager I started to really struggle with PTSD. I stopped caring about school and became convinced that I was studying for nothing. I dropped out several times, and wasn't sure if I was going to make it through high school.

Eventually I joined a genocide survivors association with other students who were also survivors, and some who had lived through even more traumatizing events. The association gave me a sense of belonging. We encouraged and supported one another, and worked to share our stories and educate others who denied the genocide.

When I finished school I began working in the social and health sectors, which allowed me to meet even more people and learn about their experiences after the genocide. I also moved out of the family home and was living with my brother.

In 2005 the government started releasing prisoners—people who had been arrested and charged with killings during the genocide. These were individuals who had been tried through the gacaca [community] courts. It wasn't easy to live with them. Everyone who had attacked our family from the region was moving back into the area.

Some of those who had been released were good, but others were not. They wanted to get even with you for having been sent to prison. People witnessed bad things happening. Our family received threats: they knew we were still alive, and they thought we knew everything about the crimes they had committed.

In 2009 I decided to emigrate to Canada, despite the fact that I didn't know anyone living there. At the time, the only thing I knew about Canada was the flag, but I was still excited to move. My goal was to find a place to live where I could be sure that my future children and grandchildren would not face the same experiences I had been through. I saw Canada as a nation that had helped to protect us in the past, and as a safe place to raise a family. I knew that if I remained in Rwanda, even if I was physically safe I would still be haunted by the memories and experiences of the genocide.

My first reaction to Canada was "Wow!" I felt in my heart that this was my new home. I arrived in Quebec during the summer, when the weather was very similar to what I was used to in Rwanda. I attended university, and later transferred to western Canada to improve my English.

My first winter was not bad. I had been told so many negative things about winter that I had built up this expectation in my mind of a season so horrible that I would actually die from the weather. Everybody kept saying to me, "Oh, do you know about winter?" They talked endlessly about the snow and the cold. In the end it was no big deal, and definitely not as bad as what I had anticipated!

My favourite thing about Canada was the sense of freedom. In other nations, you are defined as white or black or Arab. It can be hard to find a job, even in your own community. But in Canada I was able to find work, and I had everything I needed. Everyone was equal to one another, and people respected you no matter what your job was. I did not face much discrimination, aside from a few people passing judgments about me or believing that I must have herded goats before I immigrated. I had a friend who used to constantly make jokes about that.

129

My first visit to Rwanda after moving was in December of 2015. The internet has allowed me to stay connected and see the progress of the country, so it wasn't a surprise when I returned and saw how much had changed. I spent time visiting friends and family. I also wanted to visit the memorial where one of my brothers was buried. They had found his body and buried it at the local memorial in our region. I found myself unable to go; it was too emotional and painful. I hope I will be able to find the strength to visit the memorial at some point in the future.

Since moving to Canada, I have felt Canadian. I had an instant connection to this country, and immediately felt like I belonged. Achieving citizenship formalized it legally, but even before that I felt like this was my country. It is not easy to live away from my home and family, but they see it as a good thing because my life is progressing.

Recently I was able to buy my own home, which is something good that I did not expect. I like living near the edge of the city because I can see the farms. I have this dream that one day I will have a horse and a farm. I grew up on a farm in Rwanda with crops, and that has always been a dream for me. I already own a cowboy hat and boots. I know that I will live here forever, and raise my family here.

It can be difficult to talk about the good things I now have in my life without feeling guilt or thinking about all the survivors who are still struggling. Those of us who have managed to leave the country are now living a different life, but the majority of survivors still live in Rwanda. Many of them live in extreme poverty, with no hope for the future. There is very little assistance for those suffering from trauma and PTSD, and survivors have been left struggling with anxiety and depression. Even those of us living in Canada face these challenges, but we have access to support and a better life. This is not the case for most survivors, and I can't talk about the good things I have now without thinking of those who still suffer.

Eight

Rose

I met Rose on a beautiful fall morning in Ontario. It was a Sunday, and we had agreed to meet in my hotel lobby for the interview. She arrived very dressed up, explaining that afterwards she was heading to a party. I was amazed at the strength she had to go from telling her story to attending a social event. It reminded me a lot of my interview with Clement, who wanted to quickly open the door to his memories and then, just as quickly, close that door and focus on the present, on something enjoyable.

As you read Rose's story, you'll notice that, as in Annick's testimony, there's a gap partway through. At that point during our interview Rose became emotional. As she struggled with her memories, tears glistened in her eyes. Many survivors reach an impasse where part of their story is too painful to repeat. There are no words to describe the horror they lived through—nothing can be said that would ever capture it. Survivors are forced to bear these wounds as they carry on. In some cases it takes years before they're able to share their full testimony; in other cases, the horror is just too great to articulate. For Rose, moving forward from what had happened meant needing to black those memories out in her mind.

Yet Rose has used her challenging past to fuel her will to live, to find happiness and joy in life. She's incredibly smart, confident, and put together. Her experiences led her to pursue a career in social work, where she's able to help others who are struggling with trauma or difficult life circumstances. While Rose is warm and friendly, she can also be matter-of-fact—a combination well suited for such a career, and for being the role model that she is. Rose spoke openly about her experiences in Canada, including how she struggled to understand how people here knew so little about what happened in Rwanda. It was refreshing to hear that perspective, and to reflect on both the strengths and flaws of our nation.

Rose told me, too, that her much younger siblings, who had escaped the country and didn't have her memories of the genocide, couldn't relate to the trauma she suffered. But two friends who'd grown up with her, and who now lived in Canada, understood all too well. They were also the only other people who shared strong memories of her parents and family members who'd been killed. From the way Rose spoke about these friends, the connection they had was evident. After they'd been in Canada for several years the three of them decided to live in the same Ontario city; all three relocated there to be together.

It's tough to think about what each of them has lived through, and how that's part of the reason for their close friendship. But it also shows how such a traumatic past can result in unbreakable bonds, a closeness that surpasses words.

Rose's Story

I grew up in a big family. My mom was a teacher and my dad was a businessman and scientist. I was the second oldest of nine children. I had one brother who was older than me, one who was younger, and six younger sisters. Only two of my siblings survived the genocide: my youngest sister and younger brother.

We lived in a rural area with lots of relatives nearby. The village was filled with grandparents, cousins, aunts, and uncles. My memories are of a happy childhood constantly surrounded by family.

My mom taught at the primary school, where many children did not have shoes, so she made a rule that no one would wear shoes to school so that we would all feel equal. Our school, however, was extremely clean, and we were required to be tidy and clean as well. I didn't start wearing shoes until grade six. I had very big feet, and my mom felt I needed to start wearing shoes to keep my feet from growing more.

Sunday was always a special day of the week. We would go to church in the morning and then to the market. Most of the week we had housekeepers who would cook for us, but on Sundays my mom cooked and made us a big meal. Sundays are still the day I think of my mom and miss her the most.

After primary school we attended boarding schools; we would go away for three months, and communicate by mail. It was a wonderful family reunion when we all returned during school holidays. We would share our experiences with one another and the things that had happened while we were away.

I did not really realize I was Tutsi until high school. So many learned about their ethnicity in elementary school, but since my mom was one of the teachers, I was never specifically asked what I was. It was also not a topic we ever discussed at home. Growing up, I actually thought my dad was brothers with the Hutu mayor of our district because they were such good friends and always together.

I started high school in 1990, the same year war started between the RPF rebel army and the Rwandan government. The conflict began on October 1st, and in school they decided it was necessary to have a list of all the Tutsi and Hutu students in each class. This is when I found out I was Tutsi. There were very few of us in the school, and we quickly became targets for harassment and bullying.

On the way home for Christmas break I took the bus, and we were stopped at roadblocks that had been set up along the way. At these roadblocks they would ask who was Tutsi and who was Hutu. One of my friends was beat up because she had the same name as a famous Rwandan singer who was Tutsi. When I got home I found out that some family members had been arrested and put in jail. They were accused of being complicit with the RPF, even though there was no evidence to show this. There was an effort by the government to put all Tutsi men in jail. As a family we talked for the first time about what was going on and about the two ethnicities. This is when I learned that the other families around us were Hutu, and that we were actually not related to them (like the mayor). I began to really realize what it meant to be Tutsi. The country was divided, and friends were not friends anymore. It was very different.

We continued to attend school after the war started, and would sometimes go and watch the meetings being held for political parties. I was at an all-girls boarding school run by nuns, and I really loved it. It was similar to a military school, with strict rules and a schedule for waking up and meals. It was also the cleanest school you can imagine. We had teams we did everything with during the day, including cleaning and showering. The school also had normal bathrooms like here in Canada, which was quite rare in Rwanda. I'm a very organized person, so I enjoyed the structure and rules. Most of all I loved the girlfriends and how close our friendships were. We would cry before going on vacation because we were going to be separated for two weeks. We were so close that we had many inside jokes, and we loved to dance and sing. Some of our favourite songs were those by Céline Dion.

Discrimination did exist between girls of different ethnicities. They had lists posted on the wall stating each student's classification as Hutu or Tutsi. The school was located in the western part of the country where the Coalition for the Defence of the Republic (CDR) was prominent; it was a pro-government, far right Hutu political party that encouraged the idea of Hutu extremism and the concept of Hutu Power. Sometimes Tutsi girls would have their mattresses trashed or water poured in their school bag. My brother, who was at a school in eastern Rwanda, was chased by classmates with a fork. You faced those kinds of challenges, but you also had your own friends, and the nuns at my school were amazing and didn't tolerate bad behaviour like that.

Due to the strict nature of our boarding school, we really didn't have any exposure to the outside world. It was sort of like being in a jail in that sense—we didn't have radios, or phones, and we weren't permitted to talk to strangers. We would go to church walking in lines, and if we had guests it was always supervised. Our mail was read before it was given to us, and if they were suspicious about something being sent or even felt it was iffy, they wouldn't give it to you. As a result of this isolation we initially had no idea when the war started in 1990. When the head of the RPF was killed we learned a song to celebrate it, and I was in the front of the group singing the song. It was brainwashing in a way, but also, we simply didn't know what was happening in the country around us. We had no outside influence in our school. Just study, speak only French, no boys, and no distractions. It was a great school in a way because of this, but it was also why everything came as a shock when I went home for Christmas break that year. In 1994, the year the genocide started, I was in grade ten (or Senior Four, as it was called).

APRIL 6, 1994

When the president's plane went down I was home for Easter break. We had celebrated Easter Sunday on the third, only a few days beforehand. Every Easter we would have new clothes to wear for the celebration. My mom always made us wear matching clothes as kids; it is something that would be impossible to forget. Oh my gawd, I disliked it so much! I still hate my mom for doing that!

We did not live in a big city where we would regularly hear the news, so initially we didn't know anything had happened. My dad had an older brother who lived nearby, so very early on the morning of the 7th, around five or five-thirty, one of my cousins came knocking at the window of the house and asked, "Are we going to die? The president's plane was shot down."

After finding out what had happened, everyone started panicking. My mom began to cry; her very first words were, "They are going to kill my kids." We didn't know what was going to happen or what to do next.

I was eighteen, but in many ways, I was very young. I was raised in a very sheltered way. I was not taught to go in the kitchen, to cook, or to think for myself. My mom was the boss and my dad was the boss, and they decided everything: where we went, what we wore, what we studied at high school. Sometimes I would sneak into the kitchen to cook things, but only as a surprise for my family. My mom was always worried we would burn ourselves, and would tell us that there was someone already in charge of the cooking for us. We did do our own laundry and cleaned the house, as my mom was a clean freak to the point where we had to wash the walls every weekend and scrub the tile floors. But that was our only involvement. I was not used to making decisions or having responsibilities. I had no idea what to do, and just observed as the adults started to talk about what was going to happen.

My family had a big house, so all of our relatives came over to discuss things. There were lots of rumours about what was going on. It is still unbelievable to think about what actually happened. People in our country had been brainwashed and taught to be either victims or killers. It was as if people just accepted what was going to happen—that the job of the Hutu was to kill their Tutsi neighbours, and the Tutsi to sit and wait for death. Every time I think about it I still find it confounding. If someone were to touch me today, my instinct would be to hit them and tell them to stay away from me. But I don't know where that self-defence mechanism came from. I wasn't raised that way. Most of the victims in Rwanda didn't have that reaction; there was only a sense of waiting to see what would happen. Maybe some did, but they still viewed the other group as too powerful, and changing the situation as impossible.

When they announced who the new president of Rwanda was going to be, it was a close family friend of ours. We immediately breathed a sigh of relief and thought, "We are going to be fine." We believed that since he was now the president and was from the more moderate southern part of the country, nothing would happen to us and everything would calm back down.

My mom had grown up in the city, and her family members still living there (my aunts and uncles) had begun to arrive at our house, thinking it would be safer than their homes in the city. There was a belief that if killings were going to happen, they would occur in the large city centres like Kigali, and were less likely in rural areas like where we lived. I also thought that if anything did happen in our area, the mayor of the district (the one I originally thought was my dad's brother) would hide us. They were such close friends that I was certain he would protect our family.

The village was basically split into two parts: on one side was my whole extended family, all Tutsi, and on the other side it was all Hutu. The markets shut down, and there started to be days where no one was allowed to go anywhere. We also started to hear about good friends who were dying in Kigali. We continued to wait, and we began to think about what we should do if things did happen—how we would run, or escape. We decided to dig a hole in the garage, and began to sleep there. When I reflect back on the things we did, I can't help but think how dumb and useless many of our actions were.

We would go to church every morning to pray. The last Sunday I spent with my parents was April 10th—the day we finally realized we were going to die. We went to church and no one would even look at us. People ignored us, refused to say hi or greet us, and some glared and gave us bad looks. This was also the day they started to have meetings about how they were going to kill people.

On April 16th the genocide fully reached our area. They started burning down houses, and we began sleeping in the bushes. Some of our cousins fled to Burundi, taking my two youngest siblings. They wanted to take the rest of us kids, but my parents said no— they were worried we would be killed because the civil war and killings were also occurring in Burundi.

On April 21st the mayor gathered everyone who was Tutsi and told them to go to the head office of the district. He reassured everyone: "That's where we are going to protect you."

On the 22nd they shot everyone, killed everyone, the whole village died. I was taken hostage.

At this point Rose struggled to continue her story. She was hesitant to even say she'd been taken hostage. She wasn't comfortable talking about what happened while she was held captive.

During the Rwanda genocide it was very common for militia and killers to take Tutsi women and girls as hostages and repeatedly rape them. In many cases the women were gang-raped, sexually mutilated, and killed or fatally wounded. Many were left to suffer slow, painful deaths. Those left alive were often raped by HIV-positive men with the goal of infecting the women. Rwanda was the first case in which the United Nations recognized sexual violence and rape as a tool for committing genocide. It is estimated that hundreds of thousands of women and girls in Rwanda were victims.

After I was released I was able to flee and go to Burundi. I arrived at the end of April.

I stayed at a refugee camp in Burundi. It was a very difficult time. There are different classes in society, and I was born in the middle class. I didn't know how to eat with my fingers—growing up, my mom would slap my hand, insisting that I eat with a knife and a fork and sit up straight at the table. I went from living life as a sheltered middle-class child to a place where there were no tables and no shoes. You ate whatever you were given with your fingers, and you were constantly dirty. But it was still better than dying.

People came mostly from the southern part of Rwanda. Some had few belongings, some had nothing, some had pets (goats, cows ...) with them. We all lived outside, but some NGOs came and helped build tents and toilets. In the camp we were very exposed to the weather, especially the rain and the hot sun.

The conditions of the camp, though, were not really the hardest part. What was hardest was the realization that you may have survived but your family was gone. There were moms crying all day because their kids were either dead or dying from different diseases. Fathers left without their families because they ran fast from the killers; their wives and kids were left behind. There were all kinds of sadness, but the saddest was the millions of kids left without parents. In Rwanda we didn't have family names, so identifying families and trying to reunite people who had survived was extremely difficult. Despite all this, people tried to stay clean and make the best of life in the camp.

I don't complain in my life, because I think there is always someone else in a worse situation, and complaining is just a bad thing. For me, I believe that you live with whatever you have and that you should be happy with it, because things can change in a second and everything you have can be gone. It can happen that your friends become your enemies, your neighbours become your worst enemies, you don't know who likes you or who loves you or who can save you. My dad's best friend was also his killer.

I was reconnected with my two siblings on July 1st. My cousins helped me, and we returned to Rwanda. When we came back everyone was dead. Every person I knew was dead, every family member and friend was gone. You would think that at eighteen years old I would know what to do, but I had no clue. "What are we going to do? Where are we going to live?" These were the questions I was thinking about.

My cousins were amazing; they helped us out, and I was able to start school a couple of years later and finish high school. I didn't go to the same school after the genocide because I was worried that everyone I had known there would be dead. After I finished school I found a job and got married.

It was hard. I can't fully express how difficult it was. Imagine if everyone you currently know—every friend, every relative, every person you have in your life—was suddenly gone. You find a few survivors, and you try to find a few people who know you. Later the cities changed their names. This was also a challenge. "Where are you from?" You can't even say because everything has changed.

I cannot talk to my younger sister and brother about many of these things. They don't have the same memories I have. They don't remember the old days at home and what we did. Everyone I shared memories with is gone. The memories I had of my home are gone. The memories I had of my school are gone. If someone says they knew my parents, I consider it amazing. I eventually found two people who knew my parents; one of them I also went to elementary school with. They are now my closest friends. For me, I would die for them. I would do anything for them. We are together as much as possible. We were together last night; we are going to be together this afternoon. Every second we can, we try to be together because you simply don't find anyone still alive who shares your memories. They were all killed during the genocide.

I went to the doctor the other day and they asked me about my family history. I said I didn't know. Then they asked if anyone in my family had cancer. Again, I said I didn't know. They asked why, and I said that it is because they all died the same day. They all died. I said to the doctor, "I am going to start the family history. Take the info from me, and from there you can start my family history." I cried after that experience.

When I attended the gacaca trials [local community courts used to try perpetrators], I saw a man who was well known and had been a doctor. I could see the shame and fear on his face, and how his family was being stared at. During that moment I felt so glad that my parents had died and that we were victims and I didn't have to hold the shame of being a killer.

I can't imagine living a life where your dad comes home and tells you to go to school and study hard, but you know what he has done. How can someone live with that knowledge and those memories? In the morning you have to worry about whether or not someone is going to find out about what you have done. How can you sleep at night knowing you have people's bodies in your backyard? Or knowing that your dad raped and killed women and babies, and that your mom had done things as well? I live with the sadness of losing my family, but I know that they died with honour and dignity, that they didn't die doing wrong.

Those are the things that remind me I am not in the worst situation; there are really some people who have shitty lives. It is cynical, and probably my coping mechanism, but I try to put myself in other people's shoes and think about how they live.

On my mom's side, my grandfather had a brother whose wife was Hutu. The children who looked Hutu decided to kill their siblings who looked Tutsi. Same mom, same dad, and they killed their own siblings. The history of Rwanda is horrible.

When someone asks if I am Hutu or Tutsi, I say that I have never benefited from those terms, since they have been used to discriminate or target people for their differences. I am so proud and so happy now to be called Rwandan. Many people see that as a failure; they feel they are trying to change Rwanda's history, and they use it to criticize the government. Every time someone makes that comment I ask them to tell me one way in which they benefited from the use of the Hutu or Tutsi label. As a Hutu the term is also bad, as you have the shame of killing people.

I never planned on leaving Rwanda. I always felt it was where I belonged, and that I needed to be there so I could put flowers on the graves of those who died. In 2003 I visited Germany for a couple of months, and I realized for the first time that people had regular lives outside of Rwanda. I talked to survivors who told me about the relief they felt in being able to live their lives without having to face the genocide every day.

It was inescapable in Rwanda. On Tuesdays women would take food to those in the jails, on Wednesdays we had gacaca—each day of the week there was some event that reminded everyone of the genocide. That was how life was everywhere. You lived every day impacted by the genocide. Every conversation was about the genocide. It was like eczema when you start scratching and can't stop. It was toxic, and you become trapped in that life.

After the genocide we found our parents' bodies. They were in a hole with three thousand other victims. In 2004 we spent four months removing all the bodies from the mass grave. We washed the bodies and bathed them in oil. I'd come home every day smelling of corpses. I would shower outside because I didn't want to bring the smell inside.

The prisoners who had committed genocide were among the people who helped us dig. One day I sat down with them and said, "You guys need to help me here. How do you sleep knowing you did this? I can't sleep looking at these bodies."

One of the prisoners replied, "You don't sleep. You hear noises of the babies crying, of women begging you to stop, of men crying and begging you not to kill their children."

I told them I was happy to know that they were not sleeping and thinking that what they had done was okay. For me it was therapy to know that at least someone, somewhere, regretted what they did and feels horrible and thinks it was wrong.

Some prisoners did claim that they slept well and felt fine, but I think that was bullshit, and that on the inside they knew it was wrong. There was poverty and there was ignorance. You can tell someone to go and kill their neighbour in order to get that bag of rice from their neighbour, but the next day they are going to live with that blood on their hands. For me, knowing that the killers I spoke with felt bad about what they did helped me move on with my life. It made me think that maybe one day they would think to themselves, "Okay, I'm not going to do that again," or they would tell their kids that what they did was wrong and not to do it. Healing came from the realization that I was not in the worst situation, and that most of those who had committed the crimes regretted their actions.

On April 20, 2004, we laid the last body to rest. And I realized I was done. I was done with the country and wanted to leave. I needed to be able to breathe again.

I had completed high school and university, and I started to look at my options. I was working for UNICEF at the time. I started to study Canada—a friend of mine lived there, and encouraged me to consider moving there. I first came to Canada on a tourist visa, and when I returned to Rwanda I decided to apply for a refugee visa.

I started out living in Quebec, and later moved to Alberta. It was very different living in a country where genocide was not discussed everywhere. The thing I missed most after moving was the people. In Rwanda I knew everyone. I had worked on many of the movies that were filmed in Rwanda, including *Sometimes in April*, and I knew all the local authorities. When I moved to Quebec I realized that I could stand on the street and not a single person would recognize me. The first time I went to Niagara Falls, I was so happy to see the crowds; it was comforting and felt familiar. In comparison to Rwanda, this country is very empty.

I was shocked by the amount of diversity in Canada. My first real experience of this was at McGill University, where I went for a conference. When I saw students coming out of the school, I saw that the whole world is here—Africans, Asians, Europeans. The whole world is in Canada, and they don't kill each other, they live in peace. That was a shock for me. Later I learned that every country has their own things they sweep under the rug, and that Canada too has bad elements of its past. Despite the diversity and the acceptance that had shocked me, there were also bad parts to Canada and its history. I was shocked by how little I knew about First Nations, how no one talks about them, and how poor they are. That is the elephant in the room here.

Another thing that stood out to me about Canada was the sky, and how huge it was. The weather, of course, was also a change. No one had warned me about the snow and the cold. I still hate driving in the snow, but I don't mind the cold too much; I am used to it now.

I am also amazed by the kindness of the people here. I didn't cry for the first time until we put our parents to rest. When I moved here I found myself crying all the time. I was so overwhelmed and felt so lucky to be here. I had a job right away, I found a home, my daughter came here, people were so friendly, I had ambitions and goals, and I felt like I fit in. Here you can talk to the prime minister, you can vote. I was impressed by how I felt valuable. And how people saw me as a valuable person. I wasn't just another lost cause; I was someone with experience and value. I was able to rise and be who I am.

While living in Alberta I helped start annual memorial events because I thought we needed to do something to commemorate. I was worried that everyone would forget about the genocide. My daughter thought genocide was a kind of smell because her association with it was when I would come home from digging bodies and would smell bad. She would say to me that I "smelled like genocide." I was afraid that our kids would grow up without knowing about what had happened. My dream is to one day see a Rwandan genocide memorial in Canada, especially with Roméo Dallaire as our hero. This is my home, and to have a place here to hold a ceremony on April 7th would be very meaningful.

For the first three years I lived in Canada I would read the newspapers every day from Rwanda, but over time I began watching more and more media from North America. When I was living in Alberta someone asked me if Rwanda was near Jamaica. I couldn't believe their ignorance, and didn't know where to start.

In my high school we had learned about North America—I knew the geography, the political leaders, the history of the First Nations—so it was shocking to me to find that here people knew nothing about Rwanda. I realized I was becoming one of those people, watching CBC, CNN, Fox News. I started to lose some of my French and primarily speak English. When I went back home I did identify as Canadian, but I also associated it with the fact that I was becoming more ignorant and had no clue what was happening anywhere in Africa because I was no longer reading news from there. It is not that Canadians are dumb, it is that the news and information we are presented with is so limited. You hear what is local, but aren't told about news in other cities unless there are dramatic events. And that scared me a bit.

I finally realized the way the genocide had been viewed here. I was still living in Rwanda in 2004 when the Indian Ocean tsunami happened. When the news came on the TV we just changed the channel to watch the show 24 instead. After the genocide I was angry at any white person; I couldn't understand why no one had helped us. Why didn't anyone say, "Stop killing the Tutsi"? I was mad. But at some point while living in Canada, everything clicked. When I'd seen the tsunami it was horrible and sad, but I remembered how quickly we changed the channel, and I realized that this is what happened during the genocide. People just switched the channel. It wasn't in their area and didn't impact them. That is when I realized that I had no right to be angry. People either didn't know or were overwhelmed by the images. It is similar to what happens now with images of the Syrian refugees: people change the channel and watch *The Walking Dead*. I realize that I have become absorbed by this lifestyle as well.

My partner is Canadian and worked for the federal government at the time. He knew nothing about the Rwandan genocide. The media presented it as "Some people somewhere in Africa are killing each other," followed by the next news story about some celebrities divorcing. That is how news is here. When I was working on *Sometimes in April*, there is a line in the movie where someone says, "We don't have gold, we don't have oil, people don't care, we can kill anyone."

In 2010 my two friends and I decided to move to the same city in Ontario. We are the only people who remember our past and our childhood, and we are closer than family. Now we live close to one another and I consider them my family. My younger sister is married and lives in Uganda, and my younger brother is in Rwanda.

I visited Rwanda last year, and it is so different now that I barely recognize it. I was in a crowd of people and did not know anyone.

That is when I realized I don't really belong there anymore. It made me sad. I am now one of those people who we used to hate, who have become so North American. I was trying to fit in, but I realized I didn't. I didn't speak English when I left Rwanda; I learned most of my English when living in Alberta. Even though in Canada everyone feels I have a Rwandan accent, in Rwanda everyone asked why I didn't have one. It was both weird and amazing. I returned to Canada exhausted, but also so proud of my country.

When I was living in Rwanda, I felt like no one would care about me if I didn't do something with my life. I could die on the street and no one would care. Or I could choose to do something with my life. Just because my parents died in the genocide it doesn't define who I am now.

I often say that you have the right to be sad but you don't have the right to be angry, because the anger is what will take you over. If one person was killed by three people, then there are three million people who are killers on the soil of Rwanda. How can you be angry at that many people and still find a way to live? Anger can't take you anywhere. You need to live your life and move on. You can't be a victim all the time. If you cast yourself as a victim you will also die as a victim. You survived. My motto is that my success in life is my vengeance.

My daughter doesn't live like a victim because I was a victim of the genocide. She doesn't carry my pain and use it to hate the government or other people. We do not want to make our children victims as well, or pass on the anger. The story is that we survived and rose above. She is proud to be Rwandan, and she doesn't meet others and judge them as Hutu or Tutsi.

Forgiveness is a big word. I call it peaceful cohabitation. You don't have to love me, I don't have to love you, but we can work together. We respect one another's rights, we have common interests, we live together in peace. I don't fake that I like someone or forgive them. That's how I learned to live in Rwanda after the genocide.

[Nine]

Angelic

When I arranged to meet Angelic, I suggested several possible places for our interview. She decided on the public library—I think it was a location she knew how to get to, and that she was nervous about talking with a stranger. During the interview, though, she gradually opened up. It helped that I'd been to both Rwanda and Uganda, the two places where she'd lived. Angelic began to talk more about her thoughts on both countries, and the changes she's seen there since the genocide. Unlike many others I interviewed, who'd been living in Canada for several years, Angelic was a very recent immigrant, still adjusting to the cultural norms. She asked me if I was Christian and then apologized right away: she'd since learned, she said, that people don't ask that question here. In Uganda and Rwanda, meanwhile, when you meet someone new it's one of the first questions you ask, similar to inquiring about their spouse or children.

As she began telling me about her life, Angelic's voice was soft and quiet. At first I thought this stemmed from the challenge of speaking English—a language she was still learning—but as we continued I realized it was the trauma of her story and the difficulty of sharing it. Emotions overwhelmed her as she struggled to talk about her boyfriend and her family. By the time she told me what had happened to her during the genocide, we were both in tears. At those moments her voice was barely audible, a mere whisper.

Once we'd gotten through the serious, difficult part of our meeting, it was as if she was finally able to breathe again. The atmosphere and mood of our conversation changed. Angelic relaxed; her voice was now confident and clear. Like many mothers, when she talked about her children she absolutely beamed. She's devoted her life to doing everything she can for them, and her pride in their accomplishments was evident. She shared her enthusiasm for returning to school herself, her plans for the future, her career goals. Then she turned the interview around to me, asking questions about Canada, the economy, the weather in different cities. And what was my opinion of Rwanda today? Which region did I like the most?

Underneath Angelic's quiet demeanour was a passionate, intelligent woman with a fierce protectiveness for her children, a desire to give them a better life, and the strength to make whatever sacrifices necessary to help them achieve it.

Angelic's Story

When I start to talk about my story, it's very hard, because my life has not been easy.

I was the third-born in a family of six children and the only daughter. My mom and my dad were both Catholics. At the age of seven I was sent to live with my grandma, who lived alone. I knew I was Tutsi because I asked my grandma: "I heard that there are Hutu and Tutsi?"

She said yes, and told me that I was Tutsi. I had many friends growing up who were Hutu, and these terms were used in school, but they didn't mean very much to me.

Grandma taught me how to work and do everything to care for the home, but I was also able to attend school. I loved school and my teachers. I was very clever, and most of the time I was the top student in my class. Sometimes I'd go home to visit my family, but I would always come back to my grandma's house.

Life continued like this until my grandma passed away when I was in grade seven. My uncle, who was a widower, lived in a house adjacent to my grandma's. He had three young children, and after

Grandma's death I began caring for them; I sacrificed my education for them. I use the word "sacrifice" because I wanted to continue to go to school, but I also loved the children and felt happy caring for them. I stayed home and looked after the house while they attended school.

When I was sixteen my dad wanted me to get married, but my mom convinced him that I was still too young. It was common during this time for girls to end their education after primary school and get married very young, often without a choice in who they married.

In 1990 the RPF invaded Rwanda, and things shifted in the country. The government started to treat anyone who was Tutsi very poorly.

I had a boyfriend at the time who was attending university, and who I was very much in love with. Despite my lack of an education he loved me; we planned for a future together. My parents had met both him and his parents. Our relationship was official. In 1991 I tried to travel to the province where he studied in order to see his graduation. On the bus people started to threaten those of us who were Tutsi. They stopped the vehicle and shouted at us, "You! Out!" and, "You! Out!" Soldiers arrived and killed some of us. There was blood everywhere. It was my first time seeing people killed.

At a moment like that, you lose your mind. I stood there and was forced to watch as they killed—first a woman, then a man, then another man ... there were six, I think. "This is my last time," I thought.

Finally, one soldier said, "Okay. Go back. Walk ... Go back home." And they let the rest of us leave. The university where my boyfriend was a student was also attacked, but he survived and eventually travelled to Kigali. It was not an easy time in the country to be a Tutsi.

A year later, in 1992, my parents and siblings were attacked. There were many attacks on Tutsi that occurred before the actual genocide. They were killed inside a Catholic church. The church is still there and is now part of a big memorial site. Two of my brothers survived and came to Kigali, where we all began to live together.

I ended up getting a job as a cook, working for white people who were employees of the Belgian company Sabena. They taught me how to cook everything: soup, pizza, spaghetti. I enjoyed the work, and continued in that position until the genocide began.

APRIL 6, 1994

On the night the president's plane was shot down I was at home with my brothers. My boyfriend lived only a short distance away. Within thirty minutes of the plane crash we started to receive news that killings had begun in the city. We looked at one another. We were all certain that we were going to die.

The next morning we went to my neighbour's house. He was Hutu and a friend of ours, and he agreed to let us stay with him. Some Hutu were extremists and killed Tutsi, but not everyone. There were also Hutu who did not share these views and who tried to help hide or save people.

Killings started to happen around our area, and many of our neighbours who were also Tutsi died. After three days, our Hutu neighbour told us that people were starting to suspect he had people hiding in his house. He asked us to leave. Harbouring or protecting Tutsi was very dangerous—you could be killed if you were caught.

My boyfriend came to see me, and I was shocked that he was moving around outside. He told me, "What can I do? I want to see you. Maybe this is my end, and I want to see you first." After some emotional moments, we hugged and he left. Thirty minutes later he was killed.

At this point Angelic became emotional and broke down in tears.

I heard the gunshot. People came and told us that one of his roommates had killed him. There had been three of them, all young men, living in the home together. At that moment I was unable to cry, or react. All I could think about was that I would be next.

We stayed with another neighbour. Sometime in the middle of April, they came for my two brothers and killed both of them. My uncle was also killed, and I was left with his three children. My neighbours told me, "For you, Tutsi people, you can't survive. This is your end in life." I continued to stay with my neighbour, as there was nowhere else for me to go.

On the 28th of April, I can remember the exact date clearly, the men who had killed my brothers came back to get me. I was taken outside, where I recognized many other Tutsi from my neighbourhood. There was a big group of us who had been rounded up, and someone must have counted the number of people, because later I was told that there were forty-three of us.

They took everyone to the place where they planned to kill us. A big hole had been dug in the ground so that it would be easy to bury the bodies, and they ordered us to lie down in it. I lay face down to wait my turn. They started to shoot. One person at a time was shot in the head. The horror of what was happening was too much and I fainted. I didn't find out until later what had happened and why I hadn't been killed.

One of our neighbours in the area was a soldier and a captain in the Rwandan army. He heard the gunfire from his home and showed up demanding that they stop shooting us. He told the killers, "Stop killing people, these people are innocent!" One of the killers responded that they had been told to kill the Tutsi. The captain replied by saying that we were not the targets, and instead they should be fighting the RPF. The battle was going on a very short distance from where we lived, so he told the men that instead of killing us they should be going to help the government soldiers fight the RPF.

By the time he intervened, forty people had been killed. I was among the final three lying on the ground. Some people in the village picked me up and carried me to my house. My body had gone into such a state of shock that when someone tried to grab my head handfuls of hair fell out. I was described as being half dead when they moved me.

It was several hours before I recovered from passing out and realized I was still alive and in my home. For the next few days I remained in my home instead of going back to my neighbour's. Within a week the RPF was overtaking our neighbourhood and people were getting shot. We found ourselves in the middle of the conflict between the two sides. Most people fled in the direction of Kicukiro, where the government army was located.

There wasn't really any good direction to go, as there was fighting all around us and dead bodies everywhere. Coming from behind us were the RPF soldiers and in front of us was the army. Some neighbours came to get me to go along with everyone who was fleeing. I brought the children, carrying the youngest one on my back. The rest of the children clung to me, trying to maintain constant physical contact as we tried to escape through the chaos.

We spent the night at Kicukiro sleeping on the ground, and then we were directed by the Rwandan army on which route to follow to get away from the battle zone. We travelled in that direction until we reached a place called Nyamirambo. I knew I couldn't safely stay there, so I went to the home of a friend of our family.

The family had a daughter who was married, and when I arrived at the home I saw that her husband was one of the Hutu men who had killed my brothers. I spent the night there, as I had no choice, and the next day he saw me. He told the mother of the family, "Mom, even you deserve to be killed because you are Tutsi, but I didn't kill you because you are my mother-in-law. But now you are starting to bring your people here, so I am going to spill blood in this house." The mother told me to go away. Immediately, I went.

There was a large warehouse in the area that OPROVIA [National Office for the Development and Marketing of Food and Livestock Products] used to store beans, wheat, sorghum, maize, and other crops to sell. The warehouse was empty at the time, so large numbers of both Hutu and Tutsi were using it to seek refuge. We stayed there for some time, until killers arrived to attack and kill those who were Tutsi. They killed many people, but took me and some of the other women hostage.

I thought they were going to take us somewhere and kill us. Instead they took us and raped us.

Angelic cried as she told me this, with long pauses as she tried to find the words for what had happened to her.

I was still a virgin; it was my first time sleeping with a man. It was excruciating. In French we use the term *déchirure*, or "to tear." I was raped by three men. I was left very damaged, and in pain. When they finished with us they brought us back to the OPROVIA building.

A few weeks later the RPF took control of Kigali. The Hutu who had been in the building had fled; the only ones left were those who were sick or injured. I stayed there. One of the kids had disappeared; I don't know where he went, but he showed up again sometime after that. I think he had followed some people, and they had come back. Workers from the Red Cross arrived to help us, and they took me to the hospital where I was treated.

After the genocide my life was left in a very bad state. I remained in Kigali because my grandmother's house had been destroyed; there was really nowhere else to go. The three children who were with me (my uncle's kids), they all survived. My eldest brother and his wife had been killed, but one of their daughters survived. When his neighbours found out I had survived, they brought me the girl. She was only two years old at the time. She came to live with me, so I found myself caring and responsible for four children.

In 1995 I was able to get a job working for World Vision as a cook. I met people from all over the world who came to Rwanda to work with the organization. I remained in that position for five years, and then took a job as a cook for a white family.

Two years after the genocide I got married, and had two girls. It was a very difficult marriage and ended in divorce. I now had a family of six children, and I was doing everything I could to care for them. My husband did nothing to help us. He didn't buy anything for the home. He didn't care for the children—he didn't love the four kids I had from before our marriage. He didn't love me, and would hurt me. After three years I asked to separate. I told him that "You don't love my children. When you met me, you met me with kids. This is my family, and this is my life."

Angelic became emotional again as she talked about her love for all six of her children, and how her husband treated them.

When we separated my youngest daughter was seven months. I was again on my own. The other children, the older ones, helped take care of the youngest two. I was also working full time, so I hired a woman to come and care for the children when I was at work. It was a difficult life. I had an uncle who also survived the genocide, but he had a family of his own to care for. He would come when he could to encourage and support me and help with the children.

My salary was not enough, and I struggled to support all of us. I decided I needed to leave Rwanda if my children were to have a better future, and I began looking into the process to apply to go to Canada.

In 2007 we moved to Uganda as refugees. I didn't want to stay in the refugee camp there because I was worried about the diseases and conditions the children would be exposed to. Instead we moved to Kampala, the capital city. The three older children remained in Rwanda—they were old enough now to be on their own—but my niece and my two daughters went with me. In Kampala, someone came from a church group and prayed for me. They also taught me how to make soap. I started to sell that soap in schools, in the supermarket, and wherever possible to generate an income so that I could support us and buy things for the children.

One thing I want to share is that God is good. I trusted God because I saw that there was no way as a human being I could solve the challenges my family faced. The only option was to trust God. God helped me, He was faithful to me.

A friend from Kigali, one of my best friends, came to visit me in Uganda. She had gotten married and her husband came with her. She saw the conditions we were in and started to pay the rent and the school fees for my children, who were then able to go to school in Kampala. I thank God for that. God is faithful. I am still in touch with her; she still lives in Kigali.

While in Uganda, I applied to come to Canada. I decided to try because I had heard that it is a good country, a nice country. They take care of their citizens, especially children and women. As a single mother, I thought it was the best place for a better future for my children.

I remember that when I was still living in Kigali I took my children to a government school. Those schools were very poor, and it was difficult for the children to learn. My children couldn't speak French very well, and it upset them. One day they said, "Mommy, we want to go to La Colombière." La Colombière was a nice school, but it was private, and the parents were required to pay a higher amount of money for their children to attend than the government school.

I looked at my youngest daughter. "You want to go there? And then you will speak French as Faith [a friend of hers] speaks it?"

From my expression I think they understood that it wasn't possible. My youngest said, "Okay, Mama, if it's not easy to go to La Colombière, take us to St. Patrick's." Even St. Patrick's was a private school, and we could not afford it. I looked at the children and didn't have an answer for them.

I told them, "Let's pray for God to give me money and I'll take you there." Today that conversation is still in my mind. You know when your kids ask, "Mommy, we need this and that," and you don't have it? Especially education—when you don't have work, or can't earn enough money, you can't give your children a good enough education. It's a loss. It's a big loss. For me, was I unable to go to school because I was stupid? No, it was because it was not something my family could afford, and I had to work and help the family.

I wanted my children to go to school and have a good education. When I learned that Canada takes care of children, that they can go to school until they are eighteen, I knew I wanted to go there. That became my dream.

We came to Canada one year ago, arriving in June, 2015. It took nine years to be able to move here from Uganda; it wasn't an easy process. After moving here my daughters were able to go to high school, and have just finished. They are eighteen and twenty, and are now preparing to go to university. It is very exciting! They will start this September at the University of Winnipeg and the University of Manitoba. I thank God for this because this is my dream! This is my dream, and what I wanted for my children and their future.

The three children of my uncle's are older now; one is married and the two others still live in Rwanda. My niece, who I have raised since she was two, is still in Uganda. She became pregnant as a teenager and had a baby, so she was unable to come with us to Canada. I pray constantly to God that she will be able to come here, as I raised her and I consider her my daughter. I can remember after the genocide, when I put her to bed and she was crying, I would cradle her in my arms so she would sleep.

The biggest struggle I have had since moving is communication. My English is not good, but I try. In Uganda in church they would preach in English and people spoke English, so I learned some that way. I know a little bit of French, but since I was unable to go to high school, I can't really speak it. I speak Kinyarwanda, Swahili, and Luganda.

I am going to school full time and learning English. We have a holiday right now because it is summer, but I will return in

September. It feels so good to go to school again and learn. It is so exciting for me! I have joined a church and found friends here. I am outgoing and social, so that has helped me. It has been an adjustment to get used to many things here. The weather is very cold, and very different. The culture is also different, but I can't afford to not adjust. I miss my country and my friends, but I am so happy to be here now and to see my dreams for my children come true.

When I finish learning English, maybe next year, I want to move. I talked to my children because they have friends in Montreal, and I have a friend in Edmonton. My goal is to go to school and to become a massage therapist. That is what I really want to study and learn, and I think it will be a good career that I will enjoy.

[Ten]

Bertin

The day I was scheduled to meet Bertin, I spent the morning visiting the Montreal Holocaust Museum. It brought home how horribly similar genocides can be. As with the Holocaust, the planning for the Rwandan genocide—its targeted campaign of discrimination—began years beforehand. Schools became instrumental means to disseminate propaganda, a place where differences were highlighted and one group given preferential treatment over another. I've found it difficult to picture what it would be like going to an elementary school here and being asked to stand up in class based on your ethnicity—although, of course, Canada has its own past with such discrimination.

Genocides aren't accidents. They are organized, well-thought-out attempts to exterminate a portion of the population as quickly and efficiently as possible. Bertin's story is a testament to this gruesome reality. He was a victim of the discrimination that was carried out well before the actual genocide occurred. His journey is fascinating—tinged with humorous moments, unreal turns of luck, and moments of heartbreaking honesty.

I first contacted Bertin through his cousin, who's one of my Rwandan friends in Calgary. We met after he'd finished work for the day. My initial impression was of a very put together businessman with a strong presence. Bertin was warm and friendly and had a good sense of humour, especially when it came to recounting his experiences here in Canada.

As I began listening to his narrative, I was soon captivated. Bertin is a natural storyteller, and because he was an adult at the time of the genocide he remembered small details, even conversations he'd had. Time flew by. Only when he was about to head home to join his family did I realize with chagrin that dinnertime had come and gone and I hadn't offered him anything to eat—a major faux-pas in Rwandan culture. But Bertin was unfazed—the most important thing, he said, was that he'd been able to share his account with me.

Bertin's Story

I was born the third child of a Christian family with six children: five boys and one girl. My dad was a teacher at the high school and later worked for the Ministry of Education as a researcher for primary school education. My mom cared for the home and the family but also had a job making clothing and toys for newborns. She was good at that, and did the work from home.

I grew up under normal conditions, like any other child, and didn't experience any challenges until I finished primary school. My passion as a child was soccer. I had a couple of cousins in my neighbourhood close by, so we would get together to play: my brothers, cousins, and friends. My family was not poor, but we also were not rich. We were able to afford to have a normal soccer ball, but many of our friends could not, and we wanted to use the same kind of ball they used, the kind you make yourself. So I made soccer balls using plastics and rope. As a young child the experience of making something of your own was the best. Not only would you end up feeling happy that you had made it, but you would also feel proud, and your friends would admire it. Even if you had a perfect store-bought soccer ball, the toys you made by yourself were the ones you loved the most!

For me, creating soccer balls then led to building other toys to play with, using whatever materials I could find. My dad couldn't afford to buy us things like toy cars, so I would make them myself. I was really good at constructing toys and really enjoyed it, so it became my hobby. I continued until I finished primary school, making toys for my little brothers and for children in the neighbourhood who were younger than me.

Another strong memory from my childhood is of all the time we spent working together in the fields as a family. We grew things like beans and bananas, and my mom encouraged us to work hard. Even if we had hired workers in the fields, we were still required to work with them. As a kid you don't always understand why you have to do this, especially when you want to go and play. Now, as an adult, I understand why my mom pushed us this way. When I found myself in Canada, all the hard work, lessons, and experiences from my childhood helped me overcome the challenges and difficulties I faced. I knew how to help myself, and how to work through uncomfortable or difficult situations.

Growing up, my parents didn't talk to us at all about the differences or the hate between ethnicities in Rwanda. They avoided the topic, and we weren't permitted to discuss it. We would hear comments about it from other people who were speaking about what was going on, but because we didn't have any background knowledge, we didn't understand what was being said. If we were playing together every day, to me we were the same. If I was playing with my neighbour who was from the other ethnicity, he was my friend. If my teacher asked him to stand up, I would stand up as well. I couldn't really make out a difference because I couldn't understand it.

I didn't see the differences that existed until I finished primary school. It was time to go to the high school, but there was not enough room for everyone. That's when I started to understand, because in September when everyone leaves for school you find yourself alone in the neighbourhood; everyone your age is gone. So then you ask, "What's going on?" You start questioning your parents: "What is it? Why can't I do this? Why am I not going to school?" I had never thought or worried about what high school I would go to or what courses I would be able to take; I had always just assumed I would go. You don't think about these questions until you are face to face with barriers.

My parents always tried to explain differences in a way that would avoid or prevent feelings of hate towards the people who were imposing or enforcing them. I'm glad they did it that way because as a kid you are taking in everything your parent gives you. They tried to teach us about love and everything that came with it, and to not respond to challenges with hate or negative feelings towards others. But when it came to high school, there was no way for them to avoid explaining that I wasn't able to attend because of my ethnicity. That was a reality we just had to live with: your ethnicity determined what opportunities you had. Despite the obstacles, it was important to keep smiling and to go on living life with your family and friends. I decided to try to find a way to resolve the situation on my own, and began searching for any possible school I could attend.

My high school story is actually quite funny, but at the same time it is sad. My parents had found a place for me where I could study car mechanics. It wasn't really a school with proper classes—it was just training for entrance to the workplace—but it was all that was available. My parents had a friend who was a Belgian preacher. He used to work with my dad when my dad was still teaching, and he was currently posted at a technical school funded by the Belgian government. Classes had started in September, and the first vacation was Christmas. Three weeks before Christmas I saw him on the road coming home from work, and asked if there was any way I would be able to join his school. Two days later I was enrolled.

When you're a teenager there's always some kids who look for ways to antagonize and make you react. The Tutsi students would be the targets of these situations. There would be roughness, fighting, kids being thrown down. You might go to bed and find out that someone had poured a glass of water on your clothes. It didn't happen to me, but I saw it go on around me. I was somewhat protected because the other students knew I was there because of the Belgian director, so were afraid to do anything to me. But there were also more subtle actions. For example, when we were playing soccer we'd be running after the ball, and after a few seconds I'd get the message: I was to get out of the way and leave the ball. I understood, and I was not offended because I knew that this was just the situation and how things were; you just make sure you control yourself and you don't react. Some students would react to these situations and try to fight and stand up for themselves, but doing so was a surefire way to get thrown out of school. If you were caught fighting, Hutu or Tutsi, you would be asked to leave.

As you grow up you gradually start to notice things around you more and more. Sometimes you hear things that aren't good, but they also confirm what you suspected. You learn the hard way who you are, what your situation is, and how you are required to behave. What was hard was the way people looked at you if you were Tutsi, even children, as if you were a stranger in your own country. Others would look at you like you were an animal, and you couldn't help but wonder what you had done to be viewed that way.

After high school, it wasn't possible to go to university or continue with any type of schooling. Finding work could be really difficult, as there were not enough jobs available. Hutu were given preference for many positions, and finding work was also very much based on who you knew, not your qualifications. I was lucky and managed to get hired by a friend of my parents for a job only a short bus ride from home. In high school I had received training for working with electricity, and was hired as an electrician for the hydroelectricity company. I worked there for three years, until the war started in 1990.

OCTOBER 1, 1990

Two weeks after the RPF invaded Rwanda, I was arrested and thrown in jail.

It was around one p.m. I had arrived at the office, and a colleague told me that two people were looking for me. I presented myself to them without knowing what was going on. They told me they were part of the secret service and needed me to come with them to answer some questions. At first, I was not really worried; I was confident that I hadn't done anything wrong. I was truly thinking, "What did I do? Nothing. They will just ask me a couple of questions and then let me go home afterwards."

I asked them, "Can I get my coat first before we leave?"

"Yeah, no worries."

I went into my office where my coat was and picked up the phone to call my brother. I told him that I was being arrested by people from the secret service, and that I didn't know where they were taking me.

As I was finishing the call the officers came in and asked, "Who are you calling?"

"I am calling my brother."

"What are you telling him?"

"I told him that I'm following you guys."

"All right." They started to rough me up and then took me away with them. You sometimes hear rumours of these situations and these places, but now it was happening to me, and it was only the beginning. I started to think of the friends and relatives I knew who had disappeared and been killed under similar circumstances. I now believed that this was my end, that my life was over.

They put me in a room by myself. Half an hour passed, then an hour, and then two hours. The time kept ticking away. When it started to get dark I knew it must be approaching five p.m. and I started to get scared. I saw one of my neighbours passing by who I knew really well; he was a very good friend of my older brother. I called out to get his attention.

No reaction. Nothing. I will never forget how completely he ignored me. That moment when somebody sees your face, your eyes make contact, and then they quickly look away as if they hadn't seen you. He was a security manager and had some power. If he wanted to he could have just said "Get out" and let me go. Instead, he just ignored me. Even now, I can't forget this. I can't.

I saw him twelve years later. I was in line for security at the air-port in Addis Ababa, Ethiopia. I was shocked when I saw him and froze up, not knowing what to do. It took me five to ten minutes before I realized: "You're free. There's nothing he can do against you now." I wanted to go and talk to him. I wanted to ask him just one question: "Why did you do that?" Even now I don't get it. I don't understand it. I would understand if somebody reacted that way because I had done something wrong, or they didn't know me. But he knew me very well; he was my neighbour and one of my brother's closest friends. In my hard situation, how could he have ignored me? I just cannot understand.

I didn't end up talking to him. He recognized me right away and was clearly scared I would come talk to him. By the time I got through security he had already taken off, getting as far from me as possible. It was a very large airport, and I didn't see him again.

After he passed by, I remained in the room where the officers had put me. Eventually they returned. The accusation being used against everyone they arrested was that they were aiding the RPF. I found out later that over eight thousand people had been arrested throughout the country. The people who were arrested were those who were industrious and doing well. They had good jobs, ran busi-nesses, were well known, and most importantly, they were Tutsi.

The specific accusation directed at me was that I was collabor-ating with the RPF, and that because I worked in hydroelectricity I had plans to shut off the electricity and lights for the entire town. They claimed that I was going to help facilitate an attack by the RPF on the night of October 4th. I was in disbelief. I had no access to the department or the ability to do this. At first I thought it was a joke, but I quickly realized they were serious.

The officers demanded that I sign a testimony accepting the accusations. I refused and told them it was not true. They beat me and tried to scare me to force me to sign. I spent two nights there, and then on the third day, they threw me in jail.

When you are arrested you believe that everyone is guilty except you, for understandable reasons: whenever somebody else is arrested, you believe they did something. That's the behaviour of humans. You believe that because you saw the police in your neighbourhood and your neighbour was arrested, they must have done something. You don't know what it is, but you know for a fact that they did something wrong. That was my belief when I first went to jail. I was looking around me and thinking, "I'm not guilty. You are." I also continued to believe that they would realize they had made a mistake and would release me.

I stayed in jail for six months. Halfway through this time my mom found out where I was being held. She found a well-known Catholic family to help her and started fighting to have me released. At one point I was taken to a room where I was told to sit down. Eventually I was sent back to the cell. I didn't see her, but she told me afterwards that that was when she was at the prison and she had been able to see me.

Today I talk about this time like it was easy, but many people passed away because of the conditions in the jail. When I first got there we received soup to eat, once every two days. We slept on the floor side by side. It was so crowded in the cell that if you needed to turn over, everyone else lying down would have to turn over at the same time. Some were always forced to stand because there wasn't enough room for everyone to lie down at once.

We were eventually shifted to a part of the prison where long-term prisoners were held, and started to receive beans once a day to eat. Every day was about speaking to each other and staying occupied. Those who were sick were unable to survive and would pass away. You would think to yourself, "Tomorrow it may be me." We focused on just two days at a time. "I'm just going to make it two more days … two more days …" It was the only way you could stay alive.

While I was in jail, I had to meet the prosecutor. They continued with the same accusations as before but with even more details. I remember they gave me a piece of paper to sign. They pointed to the line and held out a pen. When I was about to sign I hesitated and backed up—I saw the way they were pressuring me to sign quickly, and I knew something was wrong. I read what was on the paper: it stated that I was accepting the accusations they were making against me. I refused to sign. To this day, I won't sign anything I haven't read in full.

At one point they tried to force me to sign it, and I continued to refuse. I was asking myself what the risk was. What would they do? Kill me? I was already in jail, and there were lots of witnesses around. They beat me instead and put me back in the jail cell. Eventually they removed the phrase saying that I admitted the accusation. I signed the paper and then was returned to jail to wait for the rest of the process, including going in front of a judge. This never ended up happening.

One day I heard my name being called, and they told me to get out. Just like that. It was April 1991. There was no explanation, no cancellation of the charges or information about why they were releasing me. But I didn't care; I was focused on the fact that they had let me out. As I walked down the route to the exit I saw armed officers pointing their weapons at me. I wondered if they were going to shoot me and if I was being sent outside so that they could kill me.

I walked slowly. I didn't look around. I turned at the last gate and left the jail behind me. I was about to run. "Now is the time," I thought. "I will run as far as I can." Then, about two hundred metres from the gate, I saw a gathering of people. I was scared, and because of the fear I couldn't recognize anyone in the crowd. It was a blur of people.

It was a Saturday; my younger brother had been downtown and was travelling through the area where the prison was. He had heard a rumour that some people would be released that day. He came by, just out of curiosity, and he saw me. He rushed forward from the crowd to hug me. I was like a zombie—I remember that—frozen and unsure how to react. My brother took me and we travelled home.

When I left the prison, I discovered that there were no more buses, no more taxis; there was nothing, everything was quiet. When I had left home and been put in prison, regular life was still going on. Now the streets were quiet and occupied only by people who were walking.

When we arrived home, my mom was napping. When she saw me, she was so shocked she couldn't even speak. Hours later, after the shock wore off, she cried. I felt shock as well, but also confusion over what I was supposed to do, what would happen next. For six months my life had been confined to a jail cell, and I didn't know how to cope now that I was free.

The first night home my family asked me what I wanted to eat. I couldn't understand what they meant. When I saw the meat, and all the food that had been cooked, my first reaction was that it was not for me; it had been prepared for someone else. I was so disconnected from reality that I don't think I even ate anything. I just wanted something to drink.

I felt like a stranger in my own home. My family tried to ask what had happened, but I couldn't talk or explain. I ended up going to bed, but that itself was a difficult experience. I wasn't familiar with sleeping on mattresses anymore. It felt strange and foreign. I woke up again at three a.m. Everything felt like it was happening too fast for me. It was very hard.

I was a different person after leaving prison. It felt like I sensed and paid attention to everything around me. I had undergone a transformation and was living a brand-new life; when I tried to understand it, I was lost. However, all sense of fear was gone. Nothing scared me anymore. I felt that until someone killed me there was nothing left that could be done to me that hadn't already happened.

Every Friday I was required to return to check in with the police. I continued to be under surveillance. When I tried to return to my old job I found out I was fired. They told me the official reason was that I had disappeared from the office without a reasonable explanation.

Life is stupid. My parents had spent their entire lives dedicated to raising us as solid, well-mannered citizens. To respect others, be polite, follow the laws. You live a quiet life with no problems with anyone else, follow the rules, and work hard at your job. Then your own country, the country you belong to, is the country that puts you in jail for false, stupid accusations.

I started asking a lot of questions. I asked my mother more about her life. My dad had passed away when I was in high school from injuries after a car accident, so she was the only one I could ask these questions of. I wanted to know how she and my dad had met even though they came from such different parts of the country. Where did they meet? What happened? Where is my cousin? Where is my aunt? She told me everything. Who we are, why we were living this kind of life, why we faced these situations. She shared the events that had happened to Tutsi in the past, all the way back to the 1950s and 1960s.

After this I decided I needed to start a new life. There was no way I could continue to depend on my mom, but at the same time there was nothing I could really do where I was. I needed to leave. I started looking for a way to leave the country. That is how I ended up coming to Canada.

Leaving my family—that was the hardest moment of my whole life story. I am the only person who left. Everyone else stayed in Rwanda. I wasn't the oldest one in my family, but I was the one who went to jail. I still ask, "Why me?" I still have no real reason other than that people were being put in jail because someone simply decided they didn't like you or the way you looked.

I had to find a way to convince my mom that I needed to leave. This scared me in terms of the emotions, as I didn't know how she would take it. My mom, she always knew everything; she could feel everything, and could always tell when something was going on.

One day she just asked me to sit down and tell her what I was thinking about.

"I see in you that you have a project, and I need to know what it is. It is something that I'm seeing every day. You don't talk to anyone, but I can tell there is something. What is it?"

"Mom, there's nothing."

"You tell me. It's not about me questioning you. It is about you sharing with me. What is it?"

"I need to leave," I replied.

"Where?" she asked. I explained to her that I needed to leave Rwanda in order to save my life, and if possible to save the lives of other family members. She listened to me.

"Did you ever think that one of your kids would be sent to jail?" I asked.

"No," she said.

"Once I was in jail, did you ever think I would come back home?" Again she answered no. "You agree with me that I could have been killed?"

"Yes, that's true," she replied.

"What about tomorrow, then? What guarantee do we have that our family will be together?"

"Yeah, you are right," my mom responded. "Did I think you'd be in jail? Did I think you'd be back? No. So now, whatever you decide you want to do, I will support you. But promise me one thing: I don't want you to commit suicide, any type of suicide. For me, suicide is trying to do something where you know there is no possibility of success. I want you to be reasonable in whatever project you are working on." She asked what my plan was.

I told her that I had a friend in Kenya, and that the first step would be to travel there. My goal in leaving the country would be to find a way to return to school and continue my studies. Once in Kenya I would see what was possible and how things went, and then decide whether to continue on or return to Rwanda.

She gave me her blessing, and then asked how I was going to

acquire the necessary paperwork and travel documents, which were very difficult to get. I reassured her that I was working on it and would figure things out.

Interestingly enough, my job in hydro, which was used as a reason to imprison me, also ended up being what allowed me to leave the country.

One of the tasks required of me was to go around and check electrical meters to ensure they were working properly. When a meter malfunctions it can result in someone either paying too much or paying too little. One day I was checking a meter for a customer, and after reviewing the data I found that it was defective. This was in 1989, before the war started. I submitted a report indicating that the customer had been overpaying on his electricity for the last six months. As a result, he was refunded the extra money he had been charged. When he received the refund, he tried to insist that I accept some money for finding and fixing the problem. I told him that I had just been doing my job, and that if he was happy, I was happy. He then offered to buy me a drink. Again, I told him not worry about it, and that what I had done was just part of my job.

When I began trying to get the travel documents, I ran into him again. Believe it or not, he was working as an immigration officer. On one of my visits to the office to try to get a passport he was there and I greeted him. He asked how I was doing and wanted to know why I was at the office. I explained that I was trying to get a passport but that I had been coming to the office constantly for six months trying to get one. He was surprised, and told me to come and see him the next day. I asked where I should meet him, as I had never seen him at the office, despite my frequent visits.

He gave me his phone number. "Come tomorrow at two p.m. When you get here, call me and I'll let you in through a different door."

Part of the reason I had been unable to get a passport was because one of the people working in the office was a neighbour and knew

170

who I was. She was not a friend of our family, and was preventing me from getting any further with my application. This was the reality of our country at that time; many things were based on those kinds of circumstances. Funnily enough, the next day when I went to meet with the man (he was a manager), she was working for him. He asked her to get my file and documents, and when she came into the office she was shocked to see me. It was clear that she was wondering how I had gotten in, how I knew her manager, and why he was personally asking for my file. When she brought it in he asked if there were any missing documents. She confirmed that there weren't. He then asked if I had paid, and again she confirmed that I had. "All right, that's it," he said. "Go."

At this point I didn't know what was going to happen. I knew he was an immigration officer, but I didn't know if he had the ability to sign a passport. He asked me where I planned to go, and I explained that I was going to Kenya to study. I lied and told him that I had somebody who was going to pay the costs for me. After that, he opened a document, stamped it, said, "Sign here," and gave me a passport. I remember shaking his hand, and he just looked me in the eyes and said, "Good luck."

To this day, I am really confident that he knew what was going to happen. The way he was looking at me was telling me so many things, but I was so excited that I couldn't even see it. I shook his hand, and was in a hurry to leave because I was worried he would change his mind.

One day I would like to see him again. I have heard from others that he was not killed during the war, and that he now lives in Canada, but I don't know where. If anyone was responsible for saving my life, it was him.

When I got home and told my mom I had a passport, she didn't believe me. This was something impossible: to get a passport! I was then able to get a visa for Kenya, and I bought my first-ever plane ticket. I never thought I would leave Rwanda. Never. The life we were living was not easy, but you grow up feeling that you belong to this country, and belong with your family. You live with the challenges and deal with them. Now the time had come. I was leaving.

I took my first-ever flight to Nairobi, where I was met by a friend of mine who was a businessman. He was very happy to see me. I spent my first few weeks staying at his house, discovering the city, the country, how things worked. I was trying to find a way to leave. In my head, I was planning to go to Canada.

The reason I wanted to go to Canada was very simple. When I was in jail, many foreign countries were interested in what was going on in Rwanda and the conditions in the prison. They were connected and receiving information from the Canadian embassy. The ambassador was a woman, and she visited the prison. When she met me, she told me that I was still very young and had nothing to lose. She said that Canada is a country of immigrants, and that I should try to come. Another friend, who I had met while in the jail, also encouraged me to do this. He had family in the United States and was eventually able to find a way to go there. We stayed in contact afterwards, and he told me, "Please, if you can, go to Canada."

Based on the information from these two people, I was determined to do everything I could to try and come to this country. That is how I discovered and learned about Canada, and that is how I ended up here.

While I was in Kenya the country went through an election period, and things became really chaotic. There was no feeling of security. Everywhere you went there were demonstrations, protests, violence, and fighting. I didn't feel safe and decided to return to Rwanda. I was worried that when I returned I would be arrested at the airport, but nothing happened. I thought that if I failed to report to the police on Friday, like I had before leaving, I might be thrown in jail. But again this didn't happen.

Within a year I returned to Nairobi with the plan to stay there until I was able to go to Canada. My family told no one that I had left. It had to be kept a secret in order to keep the family safe. At that time in Rwanda, if anyone knew that a family member was gone, it was immediately assumed that they had left to join the RPF.

I was still under conditional release from jail in Rwanda, and while I was in jail I had registered with the International Red Cross as a political detainee. I came to Canada as a refugee and arrived in Montreal during June of 1993.

I had culture shock when I first arrived. You leave the airport and find yourself in a big city. In Rwanda you are familiar with everyone and greet one another on the street. Here I would see everyone walking around without talking to each other. It was a huge shock. But it was summer, the weather was perfect, and the city was beautiful. People were outside, laughing, enjoying life. If anything, I found the temperature too hot, as we do not have much humidity in Rwanda. Even with the culture shock, I found that compared to the life I had left behind, everything was a piece of cake.

Then winter came. People had tried to warn me, but it was a huge shock. I couldn't believe how cold it was. I had no frame of reference for this type of weather, and even if someone had tried to explain the temperature I wouldn't have understood. I had been hearing about it on the news, in school, but I really didn't know how to prepare. My first winter I got burned from the cold. I had to go to the doctor. He explained that I had frostbite and asked how long I had been in the country. I told him six months, and he explained that I needed to cover myself up, that it was too cold for what I was wearing.

At the time I also didn't know a lot about the places to shop in Canada. People would tell me that I needed to buy boots for winter, and I would think, "For what?" I had running shoes I could wear, and they were good enough. The only store I knew of was the Bay. But everything was expensive there, and I couldn't afford to buy boots. I didn't know that other stores like Zellers existed close to where I was staying, or that it was possible to buy things second-hand.

When you move to another country, you're discovering everything. There comes a time when you have to eat, and you see that everything is different and new, and the tastes are not the same. One of my favourite things was fast food. I had never heard of it or seen it before I moved here. I couldn't eat out every day because it was so expensive, but I still ended up gaining a lot of weight from it. One day I went to a fast food restaurant, and instead of handing me my pop they gave me a glass to fill myself. I was so confused, and couldn't figure out how to use the machine to fill up the cup. I had never seen one before and had no idea how it worked. I stood there for a while and watched another customer come up and fill his soda, and then he was gone. I still couldn't figure it out and was ready to give up. I was a shy person and didn't want to ask. Somebody noticed me standing there watching and asked if they could help me. I explained that I just wanted a Coke. She showed me how to use the machine and filled my cup for me. It was fantastic! These are the things I can't forget about coming here. It was all part of the culture shock.

Another example that will make you laugh is the experience I had when taking the bus. First of all, everything about riding a bus here in Canada was a shock. The size of the bus, the driver, the people, the commercials on the side. It was all new to me. In Rwanda we never used lineups; it was not something I was familiar with. Every day I would board the bus by walking past the other people and jumping on. I remember one day I was waiting at my usual stop to catch the bus, and when it arrived I went to board. The driver stopped me and asked, "Can you please line up like everyone else?"

I said, "What?"

"Can you line up with everyone else?"

I realized then that what I was doing was not correct. Honestly, I couldn't even see it until somebody pointed it out. When I think about it now it is so funny. You know, I would just come to the bus stop and be so focused on getting on the bus that I didn't even really notice the other people waiting or what they were doing. I would just pass by them and get on, that's it. Every day, every day I did that!

When the driver told me about the line I thought to myself, "My goodness, I have been doing this every day!!" I realized that people had been giving me dirty looks and staring at me, and before this I could never understand what I had done to make them look at me that way.

After that experience and having the driver talk to me, I worked to change what I was doing. I said to myself, "I think I can adjust myself to this new life, but I have to back off and look at how other people are doing things."

One of the most surprising things for me about Canada was the idea of a welfare system. That the government would give money to people even if they were not working. I did not understand it at all. When I came to Canada the nation was in a recession; I remember it very well. The prime minister was Brian Mulroney, and then he was followed by Kim Campbell. I liked following the news on TV and they kept talking about this term "recession." It was the first time I had heard of the concept, and I had to ask someone to explain it to me. They told me that there were no jobs. I discovered this myself when I tried to look for work.

I was unable to find any work until January of 1994. I finally got a job working for Zellers in their warehouse. It was very hard, physical work and not like anything I had done before. However, it was what I needed to do to survive, so I did it. It was such a change being alone now and not with my family. I had to cook for myself, care for myself; everything was now by myself. It was a new experience. I felt like I was always running behind.

I stayed in this position working for Zellers for a couple of months. I then heard that in the West there were more jobs available. From my point of view, there was no way I could stay home when the government was paying for me. It didn't make sense. I didn't do that back home either. I realized that there were no jobs in Montreal; there were no jobs anywhere in this country except in the West, in British Columbia. I gathered the information I needed. I put some money aside to buy a tent and boots and all the gear I would need. Then I made plans to go to British Columbia in April.

APRIL 6, 1994

I was twenty-six when the genocide began. I was prepared and ready to go to B.C.; everything had been paid and planned. Within a week or two all the phones were cut off in Rwanda and I lost all communication with my family. I found myself faced with a big decision. Do I go to B.C. or do I stay here in Montreal? It took me two days to decide. I realized that even if I stayed in Montreal there was nothing I could change. There was no communication, and it didn't matter where I was, it wouldn't change that situation. I had already paid for everything, so I decided to go.

I ended up in Prince George, B.C., and that is a whole story in itself. I started out by living in a campground where the majority of campers were students from all over the country, even several from Europe and Australia. Most were there for tree planting, but others were there just to enjoy the Canadian summer. It was my first experience camping, and I ended up loving it. I also didn't speak any English, not a word. You can imagine a young French-speaking man in B.C. looking for work. It was quite a challenge. How do I look for a job? How do I speak to people? There I was, this African guy surrounded by white people in a completely new environment, with not a single person I knew. I was trying to figure out the culture, the language, the proper behaviours. Everything was entirely new again.

I had this bilingual dictionary, and every word I spoke, I was using this dictionary to find and to form sentences. What I appreciate, even today, is that everyone I talked to did whatever they could to try and understand what I was saying. They were very patient with me and tried to help.

I met a guy in the campground, and he was asking me a few questions that I couldn't really understand. I started checking the dictionary and realized he was asking if I was looking for a job. I told him that yes, I was. He gave me a piece of paper and sent me to see a

176

person who he said would give me a job. I followed his instructions; I was hired, and started working for a tree-planting company. I found out later that the man I had met in the campground was actually the owner of the company.

When you are working in tree planting they give you a piece of field to work on, a square piece of land they call a "block." What was funny was that because of the language barrier and difference in accents I kept hearing the word "black." So people would continually be saying "block" and I heard "black." I kept getting so mad because I thought everyone was talking about me behind my back, and I didn't know what they were saying. I would hear phrases like, "this black here," and wonder, "What are they saying about me? What did I do to them? I'm trying to be as straight as possible. I don't want to create any problems, yet they keep talking about me. What did I do?" It took me from April until July to finally understand what was happening. I saw the word written on a piece of paper; it was a "block."

A similar situation happened with another coworker. When you are trying to understand a different language, you are always looking for a word that you know, or something that you can understand out of what is being said. You compare sounds or words to the things you already know. There was another Rwandan tree planting and we would often talk to each other in Kinyarwanda. In our language, instead of saying the word "yes" we often use the sound "mmm." There was a French-speaking woman who had her tent near us and one day she asked me what it meant when I said "Mmm." At first I didn't really understand what she was asking, but then I explained that it meant "yes." It turns out that she had thought we were mad at her. She was in the same situation that I had been in before. These are the kinds of challenges that happen when you are trying to learn to communicate and understand others in a different language.

As time passed I continued to have no news about my family. The genocide was happening but I knew nothing. Before this I had always been in communication with my mom, brothers, and sisters. We had no email back then, but we would send each other letters. I still have them today.

Unfortunately, before the genocide, my family believed that everything was becoming better in Rwanda because of the arrival of the UN peacekeepers. When you have been in a situation for a long time it seems like it is normal and you get used to it. You don't see the danger around you; your eyes are closed because you are so used to it. It is like any other country when there is a war. We may see it on TV and be worried, but in the place where it is happening people get used to living under those conditions and it becomes normal for them. When this happens, it is the worst kind of situation. I am convinced that this is why my entire family was killed.

It was like watching a football game. You are in the stadium watching the game and you see the guy who has the ball. You can see someone who is about to tackle him, but he doesn't see it. That is the way I explain what it was like being here in Canada while talking to my family back home. I was watching the football game, I knew something bad was going to happen, but they didn't believe me. The quarterback, he believes someone will protect him; he doesn't see the danger. My family was the same way: the belief that the UN would protect them, it made them unable to see the danger. They couldn't believe they would be killed.

And when it happened it was fast, and it was horrible.

The last time I heard from my family was about a week into the genocide. I talked to my brother on April 11th. The next time I heard anything was in October, 1994. You can imagine how challenging that was. The genocide began in April; in July the RPF started gaining control of the country, and took over the capital city Kigali on July 4th. Throughout all of this I continued to hear nothing from my family.

Every day I was trying to convince myself that everyone was alive. I couldn't accept that my family may have died. I was seeing the news, but saying, "No, no, no—my family is still alive." I just couldn't accept that anything else could have happened. But I knew

178

I was refusing to admit to myself that something worse may have happened. There was nothing I could do to help the situation, as there was no way for me to contact anyone or find out what had happened. I tried to keep myself as busy as possible to avoid going crazy. I found myself doing the best I could to avoid becoming paranoid or making myself sick from the stress.

After the tree-planting season finished I returned to Montreal. Two days later I received a call from my sister-in-law. She said hello, and then told me she didn't have much time and asked if I could just listen.

"Your brother is still alive. Me, and my two kids. That's it." She then began listing names from my family, then my best friend, then everyone I knew.

"All those people?" I asked.

"Yes. They are dead." Then she hung up. She was calling from the Hôtel des Mille Collines. They had survived the genocide by staying at the hotel, but had returned to "normal life" since the genocide. At the time the only way she had been able to call me was from the hotel because it was the only phone line she could access. The only member of my immediate family who was still alive, other than me, was my oldest brother.

That was a turning point in my life. Yes, I had lived through challenges, been to jail, and had a difficult life. But what was I doing here? Why am I still alive, and my family is dead? I was questioning myself, questioning everything. I spent two days in bed, just sick—sick from rage, anger, everything.

Life changed for me. The way I saw life, the way I saw people, the way I now understood how things worked. It all became completely different from that time on. I became another person—in terms of sensitivity, in terms of my emotions. You ask yourself, "Why am I alive?" You suffer from survivor's guilt. I would think back to my journey and how I ended up in Canada and wonder, "Why me?"

There was a time when I felt good, like I would be able to save somebody, and I hadn't. I would feel guilty and question myself: "Why didn't I do more to try and help people?"

Even today, when I know the whole story of what happened to my family, how they tried to hide themselves from the killers, I still sometimes think, "Why did you go into that corner?," "Why did you try to do this?," and I question the choices my family members made.

When I got past the guilt, then I would get mad about everything, and nothing. I was sensitive and upset about everything.

It was a very tough time. I felt very isolated. I went back to school to take courses, and when I would go to class none of my classmates would have a clue about Rwanda. They would talk about hockey, which I knew nothing about at that time. It wasn't their fault. We are living in a safe country. It was impossible for them to understand what I was going through.

There was a time here in Canada when the Parliament was discussing the colour of margarine and butter in a debate. It was a good debate; I was watching it on TV, and they were arguing over whether margarine had to be yellow or white. I followed this controversy for a week, then two weeks, then three. I couldn't help but think how unbelievable this situation was. This country is so safe that Parliament is actually spending time discussing the colour of margarine. It was unbelievable—and also evidence of what a safe country I was in. Everything was running so smoothly that the politicians, including the Parliament, could spend time arguing about such issues.

It was eye-opening for me. It helped me realize that here in Canada we are really living on a different planet. This woke me up, and helped me a lot in terms of the way I judge others. From that point onwards, I realized that I couldn't judge others for their circumstances. Canada was doing really well, and the things people were exposed to and experience are very different. There is always a reason behind the behaviour of a person.

I went back home to Rwanda in 1996. I went there, and there was nothing. It was a shock, and very difficult. I learned that a woman I used to work with had been the one to point a finger at me and have me thrown in jail. She was alive. Some of my friends, who were also survivors, told me that if I wanted they could kill her. I told them no.

One replied, saying, "Yes. Do it. She did that to you. Just do it."

I said, "No. I don't want to do that. Do not ever ask me to hurt somebody or seek revenge because ... then what? If she did something wrong, I'm not the right person to judge her. Some other person will do that." Even today, if I was shown who killed my family, I don't know what I would do. I have no idea.

My brother and sister-in-law still live in Rwanda with their family. I have been back many times to visit because the country is part of my identity, but it is always challenging. I am proud to be Rwandan and of what has been achieved so far by the country despite the complex challenges after the genocide. However, when I go there and then come back I find myself emotionally and psychologically pulled back to a place where I don't want to be. My brother says that survivors are "happy," but it's not true. Happy is a big word, because there's a moment when you feel very happy, depending on the situation. But we are always having, in the back of our mind, memories that are coming back. There is lots of trauma.

If you saw me, you'd never know that I passed through all of this. You wake up one day, and your family is gone. Having a family now here in Canada—I have two kids—has brought about another turning point for my life. It has been a positive change. One of my goals is to prevent my children from living my life. They have to live their own lives. I don't want to impose what I have been through on them.

I feel that one of the biggest mistakes survivors make is that we sometimes fix our expectations too high for others. We make judgments or have expectations for those who have not passed through what we did or had those experiences. We ask them to do what is impossible. I don't want to do this to my children. I don't

181

want to take the thoughts I have or the feelings I have about things and put them in their heads. I don't want them to have my trauma as part of their lives.

I wanted them to have a real childhood, to be kids, and I think I was successful in that. Now they are going to high school, which is what I have been waiting for. High school is when you are preparing to be a man or a woman. With God's help, I'm going to make sure to help them pass through this transformation. Then I will know that I have done everything I can for them to be old enough to adjust and understand life by themselves.

Final Thoughts

Survivors of the Rwandan genocide share their testimonies in order to help others understand what happened. The goal is to convey the vital message that discrimination breeds hatred—and that it can lead a society down a path where neighbours become enemies who kill. Ten stories are told in this book, yet there are thousands of stories just like them. It's up to us to use their lessons of acceptance and forgiveness to ensure that our world will always be a place where divisions are struck down, where diversity is embraced.

Learning about others' lives allows us to see the common threads that run through humanity: our love for our families and friends, our universal desire for a better future. These threads are what drive many people around the world to leave their homes. Immigrants come to Canada hoping to find a better life, to find security and peace for their families. They contribute to making our country the place that it is—and the things we take for granted are often the things they value most about our nation. Through their eyes we can view our lives in a new light.

This was especially true for me during the writing of this book. It coincided with my darkest period: I'd been in an accident that had left me with life-altering injuries and was struggling with chronic pain, often fantasizing about death the way we dream of warm weather in the depths of winter. I couldn't understand why I'd been left alive only to be trapped in such a downward spiral. When I was forced to stop working, my interviews with survivors were the one element that gave meaning to my life. I began to learn about the resiliency of the human spirit. As one survivor told me, it doesn't matter what kind of trauma you've experienced, the struggle to reclaim your life and identity is the same.

It was through the survivors in this book that I found the faith that I too would heal. They taught me how to sift through the darkness and once again find hope. My wish is that their stories will help you find that hope too.

Acknowledgments

FIRST AND FOREMOST, the biggest thank-you must go to the survivors who participated in this project. You each share a dedication to using your own story to educate others in the hope of ensuring a better future. Each interview profoundly impacted my life, and I know they will impact many others. Murakoze Cyane.

The second expression of thanks must go to the Chawkers Foundation and Charles S. Alexander. The foundation's dedication to supporting literary works in Canada is making a difference in capturing the untold stories of our nation and people. Without your grant this project would not have been possible.

To my publisher Simon Dardick, editor Karen Alliston, and *Walrus* magazine deputy editor Carmine Starnino, thank you for taking a chance on this book. Your belief in the project, your patience, and your step-by-step guidance have made this adventure a wonderfully positive one.

Will Ferguson, you are the reason this book came to fruition. You have been my mentor, friend, and role model throughout this process. You gave me endless encouragement and placed your faith in me to capture these stories, but also gave me some tough love when I needed it the most to ensure that this book made it to the finish line. I can never repay you for the impact this has had on my life.

Régine King, I remain in awe of you and your incredible strength and wisdom; thank you for adding your words to this project. Joline Olson, Emilee Reynolds, and Jacqueline Ford, without your help providing transcription I would still be trying to type up the interviews.

Thank you, Jean-Claude Munyezamu, Andy Amour, and Melchior Cyusa, for all your help connecting me with survivors across Canada. Gabriel Mbonigaba (Mwarimu), thank you for your help with translation and fact checking, and for staying up all hours of the night to teach me more about Rwanda. I am so grateful to the Rwandan Canadian Society of Calgary for their continued support and their ongoing work to commemorate the genocide and honour survivors. Lauren Monson, Jill McDonald, Brandie Dundas, Courtney Bangen, Emilee Reynolds, and Melissa Bruins, thank you for helping with revisions, for providing encouragement, and for just plain common sense when I was having a meltdown.

To my dad: I was living in your basement the day I found out about this project; thank you for your support and encouragement through both the writing process and my own personal struggles. My mom and siblings: thank you for not being upset and for your excitement and support when I revealed that I'd been secretly writing a book for four years.

Thank you to all the other people in my life who have been a part of making this book happen. This includes my past and present students, who inspire and remind me of the incredible ability of youth to change the world. The support from my friends and family has been immeasurable, and although I can't list everyone by name, I am thinking of each one of you.

Thank you Inspire! Africa, Hope for Rwanda's Children, and Yego Rwanda for all your continued work with survivors and those traumatized by the genocide. The time I've spent learning about your organizations, and meeting the individuals and families you work with, continues to inspire and move me to make a difference in any way I can. As my Rwandan mother Athanasie Gatera once told me, "Don't ever feel small in the things you do, because in the impact you have you are an elephant." One small, positive action leads to a ripple of impact.